CONTENTS

After the Sweep **1**

American League All-Pro Team **5**

National League All-Pro Team **17**

American League Team Previews **29**

National League Team Previews **59**

Statistics 1990 **85**

American League Batting **86**

American League Pitching **93**

National League Batting **96**

National League Pitching **103**

Bruce Weber Picks How They'll Finish
in 1991 **107**

You Pick How They'll Finish
in 1991 **108**

History-making George Brett's AL-leading .329 average gave K.C.'s smooth swinger bat titles in the '70s, '80s, and '90s.

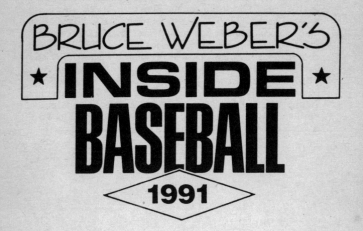

BRUCE WEBER'S
★ INSIDE ★
BASEBALL
1991

SCHOLASTIC INC.
New York Toronto London Auckland Sydney

ISBN 0-590-44708-4

12 11 10 9 8 7 6 5 4 3 2 1   1 2 3 4 5 6/9

Printed in the U.S.A.   01

First Scholastic printing, April 1991

After the Sweep

Just when sportswriters were studying their dictionaries to check on the spelling of *dynasty*, the Oakland A's got themselves blown out by the Cincinnati Reds. Though Oakland has won three straight AL pennants, the shocking Cincy rout marked the second time in three years that the budding A's dynasty has been derailed in the World Series.

There's absolutely no reason why the A's won't continue to win in the AL West. As long as manager Tony LaRussa's key guys stay healthy, his team is blessed with speed, power, defense, and pitching. Though the A's division rivals have shuffled their decks preparing for '91, all of them have weaknesses that can't be masked. So the hint of dynasty remains, especially when you see the wealth of pitching talent Oakland GM Sandy Alderson has put together in the minors.

Most of the rest of the AL West should be improved for '91. Minnesota's young pitching may be ready to make a contribution. Texas has plenty of offense to help its improving mound staff. Seattle is poised to cross the magic .500 line and head toward the top. California should be improved, while Kansas City begins to rebuild. And the Chicago White Sox, starting their first season at Comiskey Park II, think they can continue their climb to the top of the AL West.

The blockbuster trade of the winter meetings (San Diego's Roberto Alomar and Joe Carter to Toronto for Fred McGriff and Tony Fernandez) makes the Blue Jays the team to beat in the AL East. The Jays have tons of strength up the middle, especially with the addition of Devon White, who'll love the big center field at the Skydome. If Roger Clemens is ready, the Red Sox won't give up their crown without a fight. Detroit and Cleveland, among the surprise teams of '90, won't be sneaking up on anyone in '91; but both should be at least as good as they were last year. Baltimore's young arms should benefit from another year of experience. But Milwaukee and the Yankees may well continue to struggle.

The NL West opens '91 as the modern version of the old Broadway musical *New Faces*. The Dodgers started it by opening the bank vault for disgruntled New York Met Darryl Strawberry and Montreal right-hander Kevin Gross. Not to be outspent, the Giants picked up NL bat king Willie McGee (from Oakland), Yankee relief ace Dave Righetti, and Toronto (briefly) southpaw Bud Black. (Total cost of those deals: $33 million!) San Diego promised that the acquisition of Fernandez and McGriff was just the start of things.

That kind of movement is just one reason why Cincinnati will be hard-pressed to repeat in the West. One of these days — soon — Reds owner Marge Schott will have to untie the purse strings, something she dreads doing. Lou Piniella's sanity may be on the line. Fortunately, the Houston Astros aren't going anywhere; and the Atlanta Braves are, despite spending big-time for Sid Bream and Terry Pendleton, still just the Atlanta Braves.

In the NL East, the Chicago Cubs made the biggest off-season strides. Andre Dawson is the key man. Andre is one of baseball's most solid citizens. It remains to be seen whether he can help keep ex-Blue Jay problem child George Bell happy. NL rivals will have difficulty dealing with the Cubbies' mini-murderers' row of Ryne Sandberg, Mark Grace, Dawson, and Bell. But if Bell becomes a pain in Chicago, forget it.

Even without Strawberry, don't write off the Mets. The addition of speedy Vince Coleman heralds a change of strategy for New York, which had previously waited for a three-run homer to score. The Mets, still armed with world-class pitching, will make noise. The Pirates may have enough to repeat, of course, though money has become an issue for folks like B. Bonilla and B. Bonds in the Steel City. Philadelphia's improvement will continue, Montreal seems to be standing still, and the Cardinals figure to be out of it for a while.

If the season is as exciting as the off-season, baseball '91 will be super. Enjoy!

— Bruce Weber
December 1990

After winning 27 games and the Cy Young Award for the '90 A's, righty Bob Welch could write his own ticket for 1991.

American League ALL-PRO TEAM

First Base
CECIL
FIELDER
DETROIT TIGERS

Comeback of the year? In 1990 no one came back farther than Detroit Tiger first sacker Cecil Fielder. After a bang-up 1989 season with Japan's Hanshin Tigers, the ex-Toronto Blue Jay got a second shot in the American League. He made the most of it.

Not since 1961, when Yankees Roger Maris and Mickey Mantle swatted 61 and 54 homers respectively, had any American Leaguer managed as many as 50 round-trippers. Fielder reached (and passed) the magic mark on the final date of the season when he mashed numbers 50 and 51 into the darkness of Yankee Stadium.

It was the perfect cap to a super season for the man who likes to be called "Cess."

"He's strong, very strong," says Detroit manager Sparky Anderson. "If he hits it and gets it into the air, it's going to go out."

In an improved but hardly spectacular season for Detroit, Fielder the batter kept the fans pouring into Tiger Stadium. In addition to his power play, he managed an excellent .277 batting average, 25 doubles, and a league-leading 132 RBIs. If ex-Brewer Rob Deer becomes a solid No. 5 hitter (AL pitchers often pitched around Fielder in '90), Cecil might get even better. How *did* Toronto let this Fielder get away?

Second Base
JULIO FRANCO
TEXAS RANGERS

Maybe Julio Franco is learning patience. Finally. It will make him an even better second baseman, which is great news for the Texas Rangers.

At the All-Star Game in Chicago last summer, the teams were scoreless in the seventh inning. The AL had runners on second and third with nobody out. Franco stood in the on-deck circle, waiting anxiously. Then the rains came. Julio had no choice. He waited, for 1:08. When play finally resumed, NL reliever Rob Dibble got ahead of Julio no balls and two strikes. Then Franco got his shot. His double scored both runners and gave the AL a tough 2–0 win. Julio was the game's MVP.

It was fitting. Franco was in the midst of another super season, ranking among the AL leaders in singles (133), multi-hit games (52), runs (96), on-base percentage (.383), walks (82). His .296 batting mark snapped a string of four straight .300 seasons, but it still topped all AL second sackers.

Some of Franco's critics say he isn't focused all the time. But Rangers right-hander Nolan Ryan isn't one of them. When the ageless wonder spun his sixth no-hitter last June, Franco weighed in with his first two-homer game. That's focus!

Third Base
KELLY GRUBER
TORONTO BLUE JAYS

It took a while — a credit to the Toronto Blue Jays' patience — but powerful Kelly Gruber has finally stepped into the top spot among AL third sackers.

The one-time Cleveland Indian farmhand arrived in the Toronto system in 1984 with a ton of promise. But he couldn't even get Rance Mulliniks off third base until 1988. Now the 29-year-old returns after a sparkling 31-homer, 36-double, 118-RBI year, clearly among the American League elite.

"It took a lot of hard work for Kelly to get where he has," says Blue Jays manager Cito Gaston. "But that's the kind of player he is. I never doubted that he could do it. His effort sets a great example for his teammates. He plays hard all the time."

Kelly's teammates really appreciate his work habits. The first time he hit for the cycle (single, double, triple, home run), a relatively rare feat, his teammates gave him a tricycle for his accomplishment. News photos of Gruber, pedaling across the field, made newspapers everywhere.

Gruber's objective for 1991?: "Finishing better than I did in 1990." True, Gruber slipped late last season from above .300 to a final .274. As hard as this guy works, he should be able to get it done.

Shortstop
CAL
RIPKEN
BALTIMORE ORIOLES

When young Cal Ripken, Jr., was in the Orioles starting lineup on July 1, 1982, no one (not even Cal) dreamed that he'd still be looking for a day off as the '91 season gets underway. The rangy Ripken has been at shortstop for 1,384 consecutive games and has played in 1,411 straight contests. Now only Lou Gehrig's 2,130-game streak looms in the future. The other 25 major-league clubs have employed 223 different shortstops since Rip took over for the O's in '82.

Last season was far from Cal's best. His hitting dipped to only .250, and he lost the Gold Glove competition to Chicago's Ozzie Guillen. But since we believe in staying with the champ until the champ is defeated, Ripken is our American League All-Pro shortstop.

Baltimore fans have nothing to worry about. Despite the batting slump, the 6–4, 225-pound Ripken still smacked 21 homers, joining Dale Murphy as the only big-leaguer with 20 or more every year since '82. The AL's All-Star starter for seven straight years, Ripken's .996 fielding average set an all-time record.

The big one — Gehrig's record — is just four years away.

Outfield
RICKEY HENDERSON
OAKLAND ATHLETICS

If you were building a major-league ballplayer, you'd probably use Rickey Henderson as your model. If Jose Canseco is what you want your powerman to be, then Henderson has to be your all-purpose player. Big-league scouts rate players in five basic areas: hitting, hitting with power, running, fielding, and throwing. If you can fault Henderson anywhere, it's in the last category. Otherwise, he's exactly what you look for in your everyday, do-it-all superstar.

Oh, your Henderson model might well go back to the lab for an attitude transplant; he isn't the easiest guy to get along with. But the 5–10, 190-pounder can hurt your opponents so many different ways that you need to put up with some of his sulking.

Rickey's third stolen base of 1991 will give him 939 and the all-time career record. By the time he's done, he'll blow the record almost out of reach of all normal humans. Even more important, he disrupts the opponents every time he's on base.

Can he match his '90 numbers of .325 (second in the AL), a league-leading 119 runs scored, a tying career-high 28 homers, 97 walks, and 65 steals (in 75 tries)? Why not? When Rickey makes up his mind to get it done, it gets done.

Outfield
KEN GRIFFEY, JR.
SEATTLE MARINERS

Is there a young baseball player anywhere who wouldn't swap careers with
Seattle's Ken Griffey, Jr.? Just past his 21st
birthday, the Mariners' first real potential
superstar enjoyed an amazing 1990 with the
future looking even brighter. And he's doing
it with his dad, Ken Griffey, Sr., at his side.

Griffey the younger, who grew up
watching the old man's Big Red Machine,
obviously learned his lessons well. Junior
leapt through the M's farm system in a
heartbeat and proved clearly last season
that he is, at least, the second coming of
Ken Griffey.

Ken Jr. started '90 by going four-for-five,
including a three-run homer against the
Angels, and kept right on going. By October, he had hit .300 (seventh in the AL), with
team-leading totals of 22 homers and 80
RBIs.

Though his hitting has surprised no one,
his defense is equally good (he robbed
Yankee Jesse Barfield of his 200th career
homer in the Bronx last April), and his
ability in the clutch is the stuff that leg-
ends are made of. Of his 38 career homers,
28 have either tied the game or given Seattle a lead. His dad should enjoy watching
the kid.

Outfield
JOSE CANSECO
OAKLAND ATHLETICS

Is any baseball player worth nearly $5-million a year? Probably not. But if anyone is, it's Canseco who, appropriately, owns that contract.

Canseco has taken baseball to a new level. The A's right fielder is a lot more than a power hitter with plenty of speed. He didn't show it during the World Series, but his defense is much improved, leaving him as a better-than-average outfielder. His throwing arm is close to "gun" status. And he's tough in the clutch.

But it's the incredible power — and the threat of that power — that makes Canseco the most dangerous player in the game. Opposing pitchers have gone down the tubes thinking about what might happen *if* Canseco comes to the plate.

Despite nagging injuries in 1990, Jose still managed to hit .274 with 37 homers (a down year for Canseco?) and 19 stolen bases. His 101 RBIs marked a super season for most, but a routine season for Jose.

If anything can stop Canseco, it's Canseco himself. There's no question that the linebacker-sized 6–4, 240-pounder can destroy any enemy in sight. The major question is whether he'll self-destruct before his time.

Catcher
SANDY ALOMAR, JR.
CLEVELAND INDIANS

"All I need is a chance," said Sandy Alomar, Jr. Playing behind the National League's best catcher, Benito Santiago, in San Diego, that chance looked like it would never come. Enter the Cleveland Indians, who dealt superstar Joe Carter to the Padres for Sandy and the chance that he wanted so desperately.

Sandy didn't disappoint. The brother of new Toronto 2B Roberto and the son of ex-major leaguer Sandy Sr., Junior was the AL's best rookie in '90, after becoming the first rookie catcher ever to start an All-Star Game. Alomar figures to be the league's catcher of the decade.

"There was never any question about his catching," says Cleveland manager John McNamara. "He isn't afraid to get down, block the ball, and take charge."

Sandy has a gun for an arm, tossing out 34 percent of the runners trying to steal.

It was Alomar's bat that produced the biggest surprise. "I never expected that he'd do as well as he did as soon as he did," says McNamara. His 66 RBIs were the most by a Cleveland backstop since 1962; and his average, which hovered in the .280s and .290s all season, was .290 at season's end. That's consistency.

13

Pitcher
BOB WELCH
OAKLAND ATHLETICS

Here's our vote for Bob Welch as a 1991 American League All-Pro pitcher. An off-season free agent, Bob made Oakland fans happy by re-signing with the A's.

A one-time L.A. Dodger super prospect, Welch's career was sidetracked with a drinking problem a decade ago. Now, after three years in Oakland, he's a certified superstar. A 17-game winner in 1988 and '89, Welch boomed in 1990 with 27 victories and won the Cy Young award.

"Bob has always been a man in motion," remembers Dave Stewart, Welch's teammate (L.A.) as far back as 1978. "His growth in Oakland is keyed to the fact that he's a lot calmer and under control on the mound."

"Bobby has a great mental approach," says A's pitching coach Dave Duncan. "That's the key for him. He used to worry about everything — the last hitter, the guy warming up in the bullpen. Now he just concentrates on getting the batter out."

Welch always had the tools for success. Since coming to Oakland, however, he has added a forkball to his inventory, and it has made him that much tougher to hit.

"He's a real competitor," says Oakland manager Tony LaRussa. "Every batter knows he'll be challenged."

14

Pitcher
ROGER CLEMENS
BOSTON RED SOX

The last time America saw Roger Clemens on the tube, he was stomping off the mound following a second-inning ejection in the final AL Championship Series game.

Instantly the rumor mills cranked up. "Clemens isn't right physically," came the word. "He isn't right mentally, either," said the chorus.

Both rumors may well be right. But if they are, every pitcher in the big leagues should be "damaged goods" like Roger Clemens. The linebacker-sized (6–4, 220) right-hander combines a world-class fastball, a dazzling curve, plenty of smarts, and enough guts and courage to equip an entire ball club.

It seemed that every time Clemens was hurt in '90, the Red Sox threatened to self-destruct. Only when he gritted his teeth and overcame his shoulder problems did the Bosox finally put the Toronto Blue Jays away.

Though the A's Bob Welch won the Cy Young Award, a "most valuable pitcher" award would have gone to Clemens easily. He made only two starts in September, but still finished 21–6 with a league-leading 1.93 ERA, including a 6–0, 1.09 ERA in August when the Sox took command.

With a rebuilt pitching staff on hand, the Giants hope that the thrill will be back for 1B Will "The Thrill" Clark.

National League
ALL-PRO TEAM

First Base
WILL CLARK
SAN FRANCISCO GIANTS

There are a few folks — well, more than a few — who don't like Will Clark. The man is outspoken, sometimes even unbearable. But between the white lines, the Giants' Will the Thrill backs up just about every word that comes out of his mouth.

The one-time U.S. Olympian and former Mississippi State All-America keeps knocking off All-Star seasons every year, whether the Giants are rolling or merely rocking. A career .302 hitter (who hits over .300 every other year and '91 is one of those years), the Thrill does it all. A marvelous fielder, Will led NL first basemen in '90 with 1,455 putouts and 118 double plays. But he's even better with a bat in his hands. Over the past four seasons, Clark has averaged .305, 27 homers, 102 RBIs, and 175 hits.

For all of the controversy surrounding Clark, he received 2.2 million All-Star votes last summer, second only to Chicago's Ryne Sandberg among National Leaguers. It was Will's third straight All-Star shot. His single off Bob Welch was his first Classic hit.

When the season ends by the Bay, Clark heads home to New Orleans where he lives the bachelor life, except for the New Orleans food that makes 190-pounders into 225-pounders overnight.

Second Base
RYNE
SANDBERG
CHICAGO CUBS

Is Ryne Sandberg the best second base-man in the game? That's putting it mildly, if you listen to his manager, Don Zimmer. "Heck, he might be the best second base-man of all time!" says the little round man. "The guy wins the home-run title with 40, led the league in runs [116], hit better than .300 [.306 actually, Zim], stole 25 bases, and should be a lock for another Gold Glove award," says Zimmer. "Show me another second baseman who has done all that."

That's a tall order. How does the 6–2, 185-pound Sandberg stack up on baseball's all-time list? Only three players in history have hit 40 homers and stolen 25 bases in the same season: Jose Canseco, Hank Aaron, and Ryno. The last time a second base-man led the NL in homers, the year was 1925 and the slugger was the immortal Rogers Hornsby. Pretty fast company for the 31-year-old Sandberg.

A one-time 20th-round draft choice of the Philadelphia Phillies, Ryne came to the Cubs in 1982, along with Larry Bowa, in exchange for the famous Ivan DeJesus. Two years later, Sandberg was the NL's Most Valuable Player. Now in the '90s, he's the Cubs' shining light, even when the club falls flat on its face.

Third Base
MATT WILLIAMS
SAN FRANCISCO GIANTS

National League pitchers always knew they had their work cut out when they faced the middle of the Giants' lineup. "Gotta get Clark and Mitchell," they'd sigh, quaking all the way. "Then I catch a break."

No break anymore, fellas. After a couple of false starts, San Francisco third sacker Matt Williams appears ready to become the NL's top hot-corner operator. To the Giants, who made the 6–2, 205-pounder their first-round draft pick in 1986, the wait was worth it. To Matt, it was just a matter of time.

"Folks said the Giants rushed me to the big leagues," says Williams. Though Matt denies it, it seems that's exactly what happened. The one-time UNLV star made the Giants' roster early in 1987, with only one game of AAA ball behind him. He wound up spending three seasons bouncing between Phoenix and San Francisco. In 1990 the commute ended as Matt hit in 16 straight games and raised his batting average over .300 for the first time in his career.

He wound up at .277, but led the league with 122 RBIs and finished tied for fourth in homers with 33. It's a little early to compare Williams with Mike Schmidt and Eddie Matthews, but a couple of years like '90 could make it happen.

Shortstop
BARRY LARKIN
CINCINNATI REDS

At the All-Star break in 1989, Cincinnati shortstop Barry Larkin was second in the NL in hitting at .340. When an elbow injury, suffered during an All-Star contest, ended his season, the Reds' season ended, too.

That's how important Larkin is to the defending world champions. "When he's hurting," says manager Lou Piniella, "we're hurting. Barry's the guy who makes our offense go." Defense, too, Lou. As good as Larkin is at the plate, he's even better in the field — spectacular might be the word.

Cincy made Larkin, a local boy who was the backup shortstop on the 1984 U.S. Olympic team, the top pick in the 1985 draft. There was never any question that he was the Reds' shortstop of the future. Bouncing back from his injury-riddled '89, Larkin burst out of the gate by hitting .350 during the first two months of 1990. He wound up at .301, with 67 RBIs. When the Pittsburgh Pirates challenged him in the play-offs, he responded with six hits, five runs scored, and three steals to lead the Red Machine.

How good is Larkin? Just listen to Barry's Olympic teammate and National League rival Will Clark. "There's no doubt about it," says Will the Thrill. "Barry's the next Ozzie Smith." We agree.

Outfield
BARRY BONDS
PITTSBURGH PIRATES

At age 27, Barry Bonds of the Pittsburgh Pirates has finally put his father's shadow behind him. His old man, Bobby, is the only major-leaguer in history with five 30–30 (homers, stolen bases) seasons.

Barry carried his father's reputation with him (how many broadcasters mistakenly called him Bobby?) until last season. The star of the NL East champions got the monkey off his back with his first .300-hitting season. "That was important to me," said Barry, whose previous three seasons produced averages of .261, .283, and .248. "I knew no one would take me seriously until I hit .300."

Bonds entered '90 having made up his mind to bang down on the ball and use his speed to reach the magic circle. Then his whole game came together. "Moving to the No. 5 spot in the lineup helped," he says. "I had plenty of support, both in front and behind me in the lineup." The result: 33 team-leading homers, 114 RBIs, and 52 steals — along with the .301 average. In the history of the game, only Cincy's Eric Davis and the younger Bonds have qualified for the 30–50 club.

These days it's Bobby Bonds who must answer to the label of "Barry Bond's dad"!

Outfield
ERIC DAVIS
CINCINNATI REDS

Funny thing about left fielders. The AL's best, Rickey Henderson of the A's, plays best when he's happy, which is most of the time in Oakland. The NL's best, Eric Davis, requires frequent tender loving care, which he gets most of the time.

There is simply nothing Davis cannot do. He's spectacular with a bat in his hand. The world champions' major power threat, Eric pounded 24 homers and knocked in 86 runs for the '90 Reds, though gimpy knees limited him to only 453 at-bats. When he's healthy, there's no telling what he can do.

But Davis is even better with a glove on his hand. There's simply no one better at bringing home runs back into the ballpark. Fences don't bother him.

The knee problems and the bruised kidney he suffered in the World Series finale in '90 create just a little doubt about Davis. But his outlook for '91 is outstanding, if he has made peace with Cincy owner Marge Schott. Remember, she didn't dispatch an air-ambulance to bring Eric home from an Oakland hospital after the Series, and he pouted for months until the bill was paid. Buddy Darryl Strawberry now gets $2-million a year more than Eric. Tender loving care? Money buys a lot of it.

Outfield
BOBBY BONILLA
PITTSBURGH PIRATES

The Chicago White Sox still have nightmares every time they watch the Pittsburgh Pirates play. The Sox are maybe a player or so away from challenging in the AL West. A Bobby Bonilla-type player could probably get it done for them.

Trouble is, they didn't need to look for a Bonilla-type. They owned the original item until they moved him to the Bucs for Jose DeLeon in 1986. (Oddly enough, they had gotten him from Pittsburgh in the major-league draft only a few months earlier!)

Bonilla took it from there. The powerful switch-hitter has banged out 95 homers in his four full years in Pittsburgh, including a career-high 32 for the 1990 NL East champs. A pair of grand-slammers helped him ring up 120 RBIs, another personal best.

The powerful 6–3, 230-pound New York native is no threat to win a Gold Glove anytime soon. A disaster at third base (though he was the NL All-Star starter at the hot corner in '88), he's a bit more comfortable in right field. Amazingly sound for a big guy, he has averaged more than 160 games each of the past three seasons.

Unless the Bucs sign Bonilla soon, he could become a free agent after the '91 season. Are the White Sox listening?

Catcher
BENITO SANTIAGO
SAN DIEGO PADRES

The worst sight for a National League base runner? Looking back toward home plate and seeing San Diego's Benito Santiago crouched and ready to pounce. That's why he's the National League's top catcher for 1991 — and probably for all of the years beginning with 199– as well.

Some critics still have questions about Santiago's defense. They wonder about his ability to call a game. They ask about how well he blocks pitches in the dirt. But there's no doubt about that rifle attached to his right shoulder. It terrifies base runners.

If there was ever any question about how good Santiago is, check out the 1990 performance of Cleveland's Sandy Alomar, Jr. Alomar waited in the wings in San Diego until the Padres finally gave him a break and moved him to the Indians. San Diego's No. 2 man is now the AL's best.

NL runners know that if they lounge around on the basepaths or fail to get a great jump on the pitcher, Santiago will shoot them down. The fact that he can also hit .270, like he did in an average 1990, makes him that much more valuable.

But it's the arm that makes Santiago No. 1. The best since Johnny Bench? No doubt about it.

Pitcher
DWIGHT GOODEN
NEW YORK METS

Last June 2, the Mets were in fourth place, manager Davey Johnson had just finished packing his bags at the end of his season, and Doc Gooden was 3–5 with an equally horrible 4.37 ERA. From that point on, both the ace right-hander and his ballclub turned it around. It was no accident.

When Doc is right, as he was for the final four months of '90, there's no one better. We assume he'll put six solid months together in '91.

Gooden went 16–2 after his April-May slumber last season, winning eight of his last nine decisions to finish at 19–7, missing a 20-win season when Pittsburgh beat him on the next-to-last day of the season.

Long an overpowering pitcher, the Tampa native has become a cagey veteran at the tender age of 26. Once limited to only a smoking, rising fastball, Gooden has total command of a huge curveball and changes speeds with the best. When *The Sporting News* asked NL batters to name the toughest pitcher to hit, Gooden topped the list. That election surprised no one.

As much as Gooden loves to pitch, he loves to hit even more. A bases-loaded triple against the Pirates last September helped him to a four-RBI game.

Pitcher
DOUG
DRABEK
PITTSBURGH PIRATES

George Steinbrenner is gone from the Yankees now, a victim of some of the deals, shady and otherwise, that he pulled on baseball over the years. But his legend lives on, especially in places like Pittsburgh.

Back in '86, George and his baseball people picked up pitcher Rick Rhoden from the Pittsburgh Pirates as part of a six-player trade. The price for Rhoden? Doug Drabek. Bad deal. Another bad deal.

Though right-hander Drabek didn't even make the 1990 NL All-Star team, he did win the NL Cy Young award. His 22–6 record and sparkling 2.76 ERA was perhaps the key reason why the Bucs held off the Mets.

Drabek is tough as a bulldog, a hard-driving competitor. His key pitch is an above-average fastball that he isn't afraid to work on the inside part of the plate. Proof? Most batters can tee off on pitchers when they're ahead in the count. Not against Drabek. During the '90 season, the National League hit .225 against Drabek. But when the count got to three balls and one strike, Doug was even better. At 3–1, the NL hit only .180.

Falling behind in the count is hardly recommended strategy. But when you're as tough as Drabek, give it a shot.

Nothing is for certain in baseball anymore, except that Cal Ripken, Jr., will be at short-stop for Baltimore every day.

American League
TEAM PREVIEWS

AL East
TORONTO BLUE JAYS
1990 Finish: Second
1991 Prediction: First

Roberto Alomar   **Dave Stieb**

As they have for several years, the Toronto
Blue Jays still have the best talent in the AL
East. Whether that spells pennant remains
to be seen.

Manager Cito Gaston sends the division's best rotation to the mound every day
and hopes. Defense, long a problem, may
improve. So there's no real reason why the
Jays shouldn't win in '91.

Left-hander Jimmy Key (13–7 but a dis-
turbing 4.25 ERA) joins lefty David Wells
(11–6, 3.14) and righties Todd Stottlemyre
(13–17, 4.34) and superstar Dave Stieb (18–6,
2.93) in the starting group. The bullpen is
excellent, with Tom Henke (2–4, 2.17, 32
saves), Duane Ward (2–8, 11 saves), ex-Card
Ken Dayley, and ex-Angel Willie Fraser.

The outfield, once the centerpiece of the

Jays, is now a question. LF George Bell, an off-season free agent, has signed with the Cubs. His glove was awful. CF Mookie Wilson (.265) simply can't throw. Ex-Angel CF Devon White (.217) has the speed and defense but not the bat. The acquisition of CF Joe Carter from San Diego is a major plus.

All-Pro 3B Kelly Gruber (.274, 31 homers, 118 RBIs) anchors the infield, which now features ex-Padre 2B Roberto Alomar. With Eddie Zosky ready to move up, losing Tony Fernandez to San Diego may not hurt. 1B Fred McGriff (.300, 35 homers, 88 RBIs), who was good enough to chase Cecil Fielder to Japan a couple of years ago, was dealt to San Diego. John Olerud (.265) may take over in '91. Manny Lee (.243) will see lots of action wherever Alomar doesn't.

Catching is in great shape. Greg Myers (.236) and Pat Borders (.286) form a perfect platoon. This club should win and they know it. What that means no one knows.

STAT LEADERS — 1990

BATTING
Average: McGriff, .300
Runs: Gruber, 92
Hits: Fernandez, 175
Doubles: Gruber, Wilson, 36
Triples: Fernandez, 17*
Home runs: McGriff, 35
RBIs: Gruber, 118
Stolen bases: Fernandez, 26

PITCHING
Wins: Stieb, 18
Losses: Stottlemyre, 17
Complete games: Black, 5
Shutouts: Black, Stieb, 2
Saves: Henke, 32
Walks: Stottlemyre, 69
Strikeouts: Stieb, 125

*Led league.

AL East
BOSTON RED SOX
1990 Finish: First
1991 Prediction: Second

Mike Greenwell

Wade Boggs

How did the Red Sox win the 1990 AL East pennant? Nobody knows. The club was 12th in homers, last (in the majors) in stolen bases, and their best starter and best reliever (Roger Clemens and Jeff Reardon) missed major hunks of the season. Credit manager Joe Morgan? Perhaps.

That makes '91 equally unpredictable. Clemens (21–6), perhaps the AL's real MVP, should soar if he's healthy and if his head is on straight. The Sox could use at least two more first-class starters. Dana Kiecker (8–9), Greg Harris (13–9), Tom Bolton (10–5), and others are on hand, but Mike Boddicker (17–8) was lost to free agency. Matt Young may help. Rookie lefty Dave Owen has a shot in '91. The bullpen will continue to function well if Reardon (5–3, 21 saves) is sound. Rob

Murphy (despite an 0–6 mark) and Jeff Gray (2–4) will work in middle relief.

Two thirds of the outfield is wonderful and the key to Boston power. Look for Mike Greenwell (.297, 73 RBIs) and flashy Ellis Burks (.296, 21 homers, 89 RBIs) to get it done, unless one is dealt for pitching help. RF Tom Brunansky (.267, 71 RBIs) is a free agent. Look for 1B Carlos Quintana (.287), a fine contact hitter, to get an outfield look this spring, along with farmhand Phil Plantier.

While 3B Wade Boggs (.302, 63 RBIs) gets most of the attention in the Boston infield, SS-2B Jody Reed (.289, 51 RBIs) has quietly become one of the AL's best. Rookie 1B Mo Vaughn (.295 at Pawtucket) gets a shot in '91, along with SS Tim Naehring. SS Luis Rivera is solid. Ex-Padre Jack Clark will probably DH and play 1B.

C Tony Pena (.263) is a true All-Star, despite his sometimes-wild technique behind the plate. John Marzano backs up.

STAT LEADERS — 1990

BATTING
Average: Boggs, .302
Runs: Boggs, Burks, 89
Hits: Boggs, 187
Doubles: Reed, 45*
Triples: Burks, 8
Home runs: Burks, 21
RBIs: Burks, 89
Stolen bases: Burks, 9

PITCHING
Wins: Clemens, 21
Losses: Harris, Kiecker, 9
Complete games: Clemens, 7
Shutouts: Clemens, 4**
Saves: Reardon, 21
Walks: Harris, 77
Strikeouts: Clemens, 209

*Led league.
**Tied for league lead.

AL East
BALTIMORE ORIOLES
1990 Finish: Fifth
1991 Prediction: Third

Ben McDonald

Billy Ripken

The surprise team of 1989 dropped back several notches in 1990. But with an extra year of experience and a dose of good health, '91 could be better.

The pitching staff will be strengthened by the return of Bob Milacki (5–8) and Jeff Ballard (2–11), who won 32 games between them in 1989. Heralded righty Ben McDonald (8–5) will anchor the young staff, unless the Birds come up with a solid veteran starter. Otherwise, righties Jose Mesa and Anthony Telford and lefties Mike Linskey and Mike Mussina will become even more important. In the bullpen, righty Gregg Olson (6–5, 37 saves) and Mark Williamson (8–2) have things under control.

The Ripken family continues to patrol the middle of the Orioles' infield with honor. SS

Cal has now played in 1,411 straight games as he closes in on Lou Gehrig's all-time mark (2,130). His .250 bat mark frightens some around Baltimore, but his 21 homers provide whatever little power the Birds have. Brother Bill, who missed the last couple of months with a stress fracture, became the club's leading hitter (.291). The platoon at 1B, Randy Milligan (.265, 20 homers, despite missing two months with a shoulder separation) and David Segui (.244), is adequate, with Craig Worthington (.226) probably back at 3B unless good-hit, no-field Leo Gomez is ready to step in.

RF Steve Finley (.256) leads an outstanding defensive trio in the outfield. Mike Devereaux (.240), Brady Anderson (.231), and Joe Orsulak (.269) should be back. Ex-Red Sox Dwight Evans will probably DH.

Ron Kittle and Mickey Tettleton were free agents. Either Jeff Tackett or Chris Hoiles should join the catching derby, along with returnee Bob Melvin.

STAT LEADERS — 1990

BATTING
Average: B. Ripken, .291
Runs: C. Ripken, 78
Hits: C. Ripken, 150
Doubles: C. Ripken,
   B. Ripken, 28
Triples: C. Ripken, Finley, 4
Home runs: C. Ripken, 21
RBIs: C. Ripken, 84
Stolen bases: Finley, 22

PITCHING
Wins: Johnson, 13
Losses: Ballard,
   Harnisch, 11
Complete games:
   Three with 3
Shutouts: McDonald, 2
Saves: Olson, 37
Walks: Harnisch, 86
Strikeouts: Harnisch, 122

AL East
CLEVELAND INDIANS
1990 Finish: Fourth
1991 Prediction: Fourth

Greg Swindell   **Tom Candiotti**

When an outstanding pitching rotation quickly turns to mush, pennant hopes fade even quicker. That was the Indians' story in 1990, though the season was far from a total bust. That should mean good things are ahead.

For those who look at strength up the middle as a hallmark of a good ball club, the Indians are solid. The AL's best rookie, C Sandy Alomar, Jr. (.290, 66 RBIs), should be behind the plate in Cleveland well into the next century. The DP combo, SS Felix Fermin (.256) and 2B Jerry Browne (.267, 92 runs), is one of the league's top pairs, at least until SS Mark Lewis is ready to take over. In CF, speedy Alex Cole, who arrived during the All-Star break, is solid.

Carlos Baerga (.260), who came from the

Padres with Alomar and Chris James (.299, ninth in the AL) in the Joe Carter deal, has 3B just about wrapped up. With Keith Hernandez likely finished, All-Star Brook Jacoby (.293) will spend most of his time at first. Candy Maldonado's future is less certain.

But back to the pitching staff. When John Farrell went down last year, the rotation was doomed. He may miss all of '91. Result: The second highest ERA in the AL. Free-agent Bud Black (11–10) was dealt to the Blue Jays for three pitchers late in '90, then signed with San Francisco. Advantage: Cleveland, who picked up Goose Gozzo, Alex Sanchez, and Steve Cummings. Meanwhile, Tom Candiotti (15–11, 3.65) and Greg Swindell (12–9, 4.40) key the returnees, with Doug Jones (5–5, 2.56, 43 saves in 77 Cleveland victories) one of the AL's best closers. Ex-White Sox Shawn Hillegas and hard-throwing Eric King are on the scene, too.

If the pitching holds up, so will the Indians.

STAT LEADERS — 1990

BATTING
Average: James, .299
Runs: Browne, 92
Hits: Jacoby, 162
Doubles: James,
   Maldonado, 32
Triples: Webster, 6
Home runs: Maldonado, 22
RBIs: Maldonado, 95
Stolen bases: Cole, 40

PITCHING
Wins: Candiotti, 15
Losses: Candiotti, 11
Complete games:
   Candiotti, Swindell, 3
Shutouts: Candiotti, 1
Saves: Jones, 43
Walks: Candiotti, 55
Strikeouts: Swindell, 135

AL East
DETROIT TIGERS
1990 Finish: Third
1991 Prediction: Fifth

Alan Trammell

Mike Henneman

Whenever football coach Bo Schembechler needed a player, he'd simply go out and recruit one. It isn't quite that easy for Bo Schembechler, the baseball executive.

Bo's Tigers, the comeback team of 1990, need starting pitching, lots of it, to continue their improvement in 1991. Recruiting, unfortunately, is out of the question.

The staff rang up the AL's worst ERA (4.39) last year. Veteran Jack Morris (15–18, an ugly 4.51) was hit early and often. Jeff Robinson (10–9, 5.96) and Frank Tanana (9–8, 5.31) were even worse. Youngsters like lefties Steve Searcy (2–7, 4.66, and streaks of wildness) and Scott Aldred (1–2, 3.77) might take over. Ex-Astro Bill Gullickson may help.

The bullpen is in much better shape. Lefty Jerry Don Gleaton (1–3, 2.94, 13 saves) was a find, and Mike Henneman (8–6, 22 saves) is solid. Overall, the AL's busiest 'pen was 24–15 with 45 saves.

Can 1B Cecil Fielder (.277, 51 homers, 132 RBIs) possibly duplicate his near-miss MVP '90 season? Probably not. But ex-Brewer Rob Deer (27 homers but lots of strikeouts) should thrive in Detroit and keep opponents from pitching around Fielder, which would help a lot. SS Alan Trammell (.304, 89 RBIs) joins Fielder and Deer to produce outstanding punch.

Travis Fryman (.297), who had never played third base before last July, shows promise of becoming a terrific 3B — soon. CF Mike Cuyler arrived last September and bounced Lloyd Moseby (.248) over to left. Utility man Tony Phillips set career highs in hits, RBIs, runs, and steals. 2B Lou Whitaker (.237, lowest since '80) may be backsliding. Mike Heath and Mark Salas form a solid one-two combo behind the plate.

STAT LEADERS — 1990

BATTING
Average: Trammell, .304
Runs: Fielder, 104
Hits: Trammell, 170
Doubles: Trammell, 37
Triples: Phillips, Moseby, 5
Home runs: Fielder, 51*
RBIs: Fielder, 132*
Stolen bases: Phillips, 19

PITCHING
Wins: Morris, 15
Losses: Morris, 18
Complete games:
    Morris, 11**
Shutouts: Morris, 3
Saves: Henneman, 22
Walks: Morris, 97
Strikeouts: Morris, 162

*Led league.
**Tied for league lead.

AL East
NEW YORK YANKEES
1990 Finish: Seventh
1991 Prediction: Sixth

Roberto Kelly

Kevin Maas

In year 1 A.G. (after George), the Yankees must begin building from the bottom of the standings. Fortunately, the AL East isn't overpowering. Unfortunately, the Yankees are even worse.

Naturally, the return of a healthy 1B Don Mattingly (.256, 5 homers) would help enormously. Nice-guy Donnie came off the DL last September and showed he could still play baseball. Whether his back can hold up for a whole pounding season is another question. Either way, the Yanks must find a spot for young Kevin Maas (.252, 21 homers in only 254 at-bats), who filled in while Mattingly was down last summer. The club is set with steady 2B Steve Sax (only .260) and SS Alvaro Espinoza (.224). But 3B is another problem, one which may only be solved with a free-agent signing. Otherwise, Jim Leyritz (.257) or Randy Velarde (.210) will get the call again.

CF Roberto Kelly (.285) might be the Yanks' No. 1 player these days. Jesse Barfield (.246, 78 RBIs) is set in right, if he wants it. LF is being turned over to rookie Bam-Bam Meulens, a minor-league star, unless Mel Hall is back.

Despite only 29 starts, Rick Cerone (.302) should remain a solid backup to Bob Geren (.213), a strong-throwing catcher.

The mound staff is in total disarray. The team ERA was 12th in the AL in '90, and the only help on the way comes from rookies Dave Eiland (2–1) and Steve Adkins (1–2, 6.38). Starter Tim Leary (9–19, but a lot better than that) re-signed for three years. Ex-Royal Steve Farr (13–7, 1.98) should help, and just in time as relief ace Dave Righetti (1–1, 36 saves) left for San Francisco. Andy Hawkins (5–12) of lost no-hitter fame should be back, along with Lee Guetterman (11–7).

STAT LEADERS — 1990

BATTING
Average: Kelly, .285
Runs: Kelly, 85
Hits: Kelly, 183
Doubles: Kelly, 32
Triples: Kelly, 4
Home runs: Barfield, 25
RBIs: Barfield, 78
Stolen bases: Sax, 43

PITCHING
Wins: Guetterman, 11
Losses: Leary, 19*
Complete games:
    Leary, 6
Shutouts: Three with 1
Saves: Righetti, 36
Walks: Hawkins, 82
Strikeouts: Leary, 138

*Led league.

AL East
MILWAUKEE BREWERS
1990 Finish: Sixth
1991 Prediction: Seventh

Dan Plesac **Gary Sheffield**

Milwaukee manager Tom Trebelhorn is on the hot seat — and he knows it. The Brewers, expected to challenge in the AL East last year, flopped miserably, led by 1989 MVP Robin Yount's nosedive from .318 to .247. A turnaround by the Brewer all-timer is the first step toward another pennant drive.

Trebelhorn will start building with a solid left side of the infield. One-time Gatorade HS Player of the Year Gary Sheffield (.294, 67 RBIs) has shown that he's a legitimate major-leaguer at 3B. Young Bill Spiers (.242) enjoys great range at SS. If vet 1B-2B Paul Molitor (.285), who missed 59 games with shoulder problems in '90, is ready in '91, Trebelhorn will sleep better. Jimmy Gantner (.263) got most of the action at second last year, with Greg Brock (.248) now challenged by George Canale at 1B.

Unhappy free-agent OF Rob Deer (27 homers) signed with Detroit. Disappointing Mike Felder (.274) and Greg Vaughn (.220) figure to surround Yount in the outfield. Powerful Franklin Stubbs said goodbye to the Astros and hello to the Brewers. He'll provide needed power. If not, Milwaukee will probably have to trade for a power-hitting OF.

B.J. Surhoff (.276), despite defensive weaknesses, will be the No. 1 catcher, with young Tim McIntosh backing up.

Lefty Teddy Higuera (11–10, 3.76) an off-season free agent, re-signed with the Brew Crew for another four years. Righty Ron Robinson (12–5, 2.91) was a pleasant surprise in '90, along with Chris Bosio (4–9), Mark Knudson (10–9), and Jaime Navarro (8–7). Lefties Narciso Elvira and Kevin Brown could find spots this season. Longtime bullpen boss Dan Plesac (3–7, 24 saves) could be dealt.

STAT LEADERS — 1990

BATTING
Average: Sheffield, .294
Runs: Yount, 98
Hits: Parker, 176
Doubles: Sheffield, Parker, 30
Triples: Molitor, 6
Home runs: Deer, 27
RBIs: Parker, 92
Stolen bases: Sheffield, 25

PITCHING
Wins: Robinson, 12
Losses: Higuera, 10
Complete games: Robinson, 7
Shutouts: Robinson, Knudson, 2
Saves: Plesac, 24
Walks: Krueger, 54
Strikeouts: Higuera, 129

AL West
OAKLAND ATHLETICS
1990 Finish: First
1991 Prediction: First

Carney Lansford

Dave Stewart

In Oakland, where aftershocks usually follow earthquakes, the town hasn't stopped shaking since the Cincinnati sweep shelved the Athletics' dynasty talk. Still, another Series shot is well within their grasp.

Every manager in baseball would gladly swap problems with manager-lawyer Tony LaRussa. Can he survive Mike Gallego (good field, little hit) at 2B? He has baseball's best outfield: RF Jose Canseco, LF Rickey Henderson, and CFs Dave Henderson and ex-Royal Willie Wilson. Rickey (.325, 28 homers, 65 stolen bases), maybe the best leadoff hitter ever and shortly the all-time steals leader, seems happy in Oakland — but for how long? The all-powerful Canseco (.274, 37 homers, 101 RBIs in only 131 games) scares opponents with his power and scares Oakland with his sore back. Dave Henderson (.271) and Wilson are aging. Tough problem? Not really — especially with Harold Baines (.284) around as the DH.

A healthy SS Walt Weiss (.265) rejoins slugging 1B Mark McGwire (.235, 35 homers, 108 RBIs), hitting specialist 3B Carney Lansford, and Gallego at 2B. Terry Steinbach and free-agent Ron Hassey are tops behind the dish.

Pitching? Wow! Although free-agent Scott Sanderson (17–11) is gone, Oakland still has four-time 20-game winner Dave Stewart (22–11), Cy Young-winner Bob Welch (27–6), Curt Young (9–6), and Mike Moore (13–15) to form a rock-solid starting rotation. Control king Dennis Eckersley (4–2, 48 saves, though rocked in the Series) keys an outstanding bullpen.

STAT LEADERS — 1990

BATTING
Average: R. Henderson, .325
Runs: R. Henderson, 119*
Hits: R. Henderson, 159
Doubles: R. Henderson, 33
Triples: R. Henderson, Randolph, 3
Home runs: McGwire, 39
RBIs: McGwire, 108
Stolen bases: R. Henderson, 65*

PITCHING
Wins: Welch, 27*
Losses: Moore, 15
Complete games: Stewart, 11**
Shutouts: Stewart, 4**
Saves: Eckersley, 48
Walks: Moore, 84
Strikeouts: Stewart, 166

*Led league.
**Tied for league lead.

AL West
TEXAS RANGERS
1990 Finish: Third
1991 Prediction: Second

Nolan Ryan　　　　　　　　　**Rafael Palmeiro**

"The Oakland Athletics," sighed Texas manager Bobby Valentine. "They keep making it hard for all of us in the AL West." True enough, but except for a horrid month of May, Valentine's 1990 Rangers might have made it hard for the champion A's.

Thanks in large measure to a huge turnaround by right-hander Bobby Witt (17–10, 7 complete games, 3.36 ERA, 221 strikeouts; all career highs), the pitching staff seems to be in excellent shape. Of course, that requires Nolan Ryan (13–9, 3.44, 232 strikeouts) to be as good at age 44 as he was at 43. Why not? Right-hander Kevin Brown (12–10, 3.60) continues to improve. The bullpen, led by closers Kenny Rogers (10–6, 15 saves) and Jeff Russell (1–5, 10 saves), won 23 games, had 36 saves, and enjoyed a 3.48

ERA in '90. Valentine may gamble by throwing Rogers into the rotation in '91. Look for righties Scott Chiamparino (an ex-Athletic) and Gerald Alexander to get full shots at the Ranger staff this spring. There will be loads of opportunities.

Hitting star 1B Rafael Palmeiro (.319, 191 league-leading hits) paces an up-and-down infield group. All-Pro 2B Julio Franco (.296, 69 RBIs) is a definite up, though he occasionally loses his focus. Steve Buechele (.215) should return at 3B. Despite knee problems, Jeff Huson (.240) should replace departed Jeff Kunkel at short.

Kevin Belcher (.293 at Tulsa) joins the hunt for an outfield job, where Ruben Sierra (.280, 16 homers, 96 RBIs) is the key guy. Gary Pettis (.239) is on the downside, and Pete Incaviglia (.233, 24 homers, 85 RBIs) is prime trade bait. The adequate catching picture includes ex-Padre Mark Parent (.222) and vets Geno Petralli (.255) and Mike Stanley (.249).

STAT LEADERS — 1990

BATTING
Average: Palmeiro, .319
Runs: Franco, 96
Hits: Palmeiro, 191*
Doubles: Sierra, 37
Triples: Pettis, 8
Home runs: Incaviglia, 24
RBIs: Sierra, 96
Stolen bases: Pettis, 38

PITCHING
Wins: Witt, 17
Losses: Hough, 12
Complete games: Witt, 7
Shutouts: Ryan,
    Brown, 2
Saves: Rogers, 15
Walks: Hough, 119
Strikeouts: Ryan, 232*

*Led league.

AL West
CHICAGO WHITE SOX
1990 Finish: Second
1991 Prediction: Third

Carlton Fisk

Bobby Thigpen

Jeff Torborg's White Sox won 94 games, 25 more than they had in 1989. Now, the AL manager of the year must do it again — in front of the huge crowds that will pack Comiskey Park II, which opens this spring.

Gentleman Jeff has an outstanding young infield, an even younger pitching staff, and the oldest catcher in major-league captivity.

Frank Thomas (.330 in 60 late-season games) starts his third year of pro ball as the AL's most promising first sacker. 2B Scott Fletcher hit .242 but finished second only to Detroit's Lou Whitaker in fielding (nine errors all season). SS Ozzie Guillen (.279), the Sox captain, will try to put together back-to-back All-Star seasons; and 3B Robin Ventura (.249), the ex-Olympian, aims for consistency in his second full season.

There's good speed and defense in the outfield, with Lance Johnson (.285, 51 RBIs) surrounded by Sammy Sosa (.233) and newcomer Tim Raines (.287, 49 steals). Since Comiskey II is bigger than the original model, more power will be required. The Sox may get it from ex-Indian Cory Snyder.

Ancient (well, 43 anyway) Pudge Fisk (.285, 18 homers, 65 RBIs) should be back behind the plate, which is great news for Torborg's too-young-to-shave starting pitchers. Alex Fernandez (5–5) got to the big club just two months after being drafted out of Miami-Dade Jr. College. He may be the most talented of a bunch that includes Greg Hibbard (14–9) and Melido "No Hit" Perez (13–14). They can get very comfortable knowing that baseball's single-season save king, Bobby Thigpen (4–6, 57 saves), works behind them.

The Sox might not be able to duplicate '90 or catch the A's. But '91 will be fun.

STAT LEADERS — 1990

BATTING

Average: Fisk,
  Johnson, .285
Runs: Calderon, 85
Hits: Calderon, 166
Doubles: Calderon, 44
Triples: Sosa, 10
Home runs: Fisk, 18
RBIs: Calderon, 74
Stolen bases: Johnson, 36

PITCHING

Wins: McDowell,
  Hibbard, 14
Losses: Perez, 14
Complete games:
  McDowell, 4
Shutouts: Perez, 3
Saves: Thigpen, 57*
Walks: Perez, 86
Strikeouts: McDowell, 165

*Led league.

AL West
SEATTLE MARINERS
1990 Finish: Fifth
1991 Prediction: Fourth

Harold Reynolds

Erik Hanson

Seattle has never (repeat, never) had a winning season. This could be it. If the pitching continues to flourish and the hitting improves, this could be the year.

It should. In OF Ken Griffey, Jr. (.300, 22 homers, 80 RBIs), the M's have a young player to build a franchise around. In OF Ken Griffey, Sr., the M's have a father-leader to bring out the best in junior — and his teammates. 1B Tino Martinez is ready to take over in Seattle, which will create problems for Alvin Davis (.283, 17 homers) and Pete O'Brien (.224), who played first for most of '90. Look for Davis to do lots of DH-ing.

2B Harold Reynolds (.252) is among the AL's best, and 3B Edgar Martinez (.302, but a leaky glove) was a pleasant surprise last season. Omar Vizquel (.247) figures to return at shortstop.

Besides young Griffey, the outfield will likely employ a committee setup again in '91, with Henry Cotto (.259) and Greg Briley (.246) getting most of the action. C Dave Valle (.214) is good enough defensively that the M's can afford to carry his bat.

Huge Randy "No Hit" Johnson (14–11, 3.65) is a key to the mound staff whose team ERA was the AL's third best in '90. Erik Hanson (18–9, 3.24), who had the best season ever for a Mariner righty, and Brian Holman (11–11) help complete the rotation, with Matt Young (8–18, 3.51, after a horrid 1–7 start) having departed for Fenway Park. The bullpen is fairly well equipped, with Mike Schooler (1–4, but 2.25 and 30 saves) rapidly becoming a premier closer.

Manager Jim Lefebvre came to the M's manager's job after a career as a top-flight hitting coach. His best performance will make Seattle a winner.

STAT LEADERS — 1990

BATTING	PITCHING
Average: Martinez, .302	Wins: Hanson, 18
Runs: Reynolds, 100	Losses: Young, 18
Hits: Griffey, Jr., 179	Complete games:
Doubles: Reynolds, 36	Young, 7
Triples: Griffey, Jr., 7	Shutouts: Johnson, 2
Home runs: Griffey, Jr., 22	Saves: Schooler, 30
RBIs: Griffey, Jr., 80	Walks: Johnson, 120*
Stolen bases: Reynolds, 31	Strikeouts: Hanson, 211

*Led league.

AL West
CALIFORNIA ANGELS
1990 Finish: Fourth
1991 Prediction: Fifth

Jim Abbott

Chuck Finley

You figure it out. The California Angels spend $16-million to sign the AL's best left-hander, Mark Langston, and he goes 10–17 with a horrid 4.40 ERA. Meanwhile, lefty Chuck Finley (18–9, 2.40) becomes the AL's new best southpaw. That, of course, is why teams play 162 games a year. Bottom line: If Langston bounces back — and he should — the Angels could have the best pitching staff in the league.

That could make summer '91 a lot more pleasant for manager Doug Rader, who can also turn to storybook lefty Jim Abbott (10–14, 4.51) and right-hander Kirk McCaskill (12–11, 3.25). Rader's bullpen isn't bad, either. Righties Mark Eichhorn (2–5, 13 saves) and Bryan Harvey (4–4, 25 saves) are solid closers, but middle-reliever Willie Fraser (5–4,

3.08) was traded to the Blue Jays.

Things are getting crowded in the Angel outfield with RF Dave Winfield (.267, 21 homers, 78 RBIs) and LF Luis Polonia (.335, with a weak glove) fairly well set. Dante Bichette (.255) and Chili Davis (.265) are also available. Young Lee Stevens (.214) and vet Wally Joyner (.268) both deserve playing time, but there's only one first baseman and no room in the outfield. CF Devon White was traded to Toronto for Junior Felix (.263). The DH spot might have been open for an extra outfielder, but free-agent Brian Downing (.273) rallied late last season.

Though Joyner-Stevens should be at first, Johnny Ray (.277) has slipped at 2B. SS Dick Schofield (.255) missed two months with injuries, and 3B Jack Howell (.228) forgot how to catch the ball. Rick Schu (.268) should play a major role in '91. Lance Parrish (.268) remains one of the AL's top backstops.

A healthy Langston and improved offense could pay off handsomely for the Halos.

STAT LEADERS — 1990

BATTING
Average: Polonia, .335
Runs: Winfield, 70
Hits: Polonia, 135
Doubles: Ray, 23
Triples: Polonia, 9
Home runs: Parrish, 24
RBIs: Winfield, 78
Stolen bases: White, Polonia, 21

PITCHING
Wins: Finley, 18
Losses: Langston, 17
Complete games: Finley, 7
Shutouts: Finley, 2
Saves: Harvey, 25
Walks: Langston, 104
Strikeouts: Langston, 195

AL West
MINNESOTA TWINS
1990 Finish: Seventh
1991 Prediction: Sixth

Kirby Puckett   **Kent Hrbek**

Twins manager Tom Kelly has a problem: His pitching is young; his power is aging. Will the power still be powerful when the pitching is dominating? CF Kirby Puckett, for one, certainly hopes so. Memories of the 1987 World Series win still keep the round man going.

Kelly would like to have a new veteran arm to add to his kiddy mound corps. If so, the newcomer will join youngsters like right-hander Kevin Tapani (12–8), the Twins' only double-figures winner in '90; right-hander Scott Erickson (8–4, 2.87); lefty Allan Anderson (a most disappointing 7–18, 4.53); and southpaw Mark Guthrie (7—9). Ex-Met hotshot David West? The big lefty (7–9 in '90) will have to fight for his job.

The Twins believe that either ex-Giant

Steve Bedrosian (9–9, 4.20, 17 saves) or minor-league reliever of the year, hard-throwing Rich Garces, will be their closer. That would move Rick Aguilera (5–3, 2.76, 32 saves) into the starting rotation. Not bad.

The Twins hit only 100 homers last year, pitiful for any team that calls the Humphrey Homerdome home. CF Puckett (.298, only 12 homers, 80 RBIs) slipped a couple of pegs; so did 1B Kent Hrbek (.287, 22 homers, 79 RBIs). 3B Gary Gaetti, an off-season free agent, hit only .229, but with 16 round-trippers and 85 RBIs. Chuck Knoblauch could take over at 2B, possibly replacing Al Newman (.242) and Nelson Liriano.

OF Shane Mack (.326) finally looks like a hitter, but there are problems in right where Randy Bush (.243) and Carmen Castillo (.219) have worked. C Brian Harper's glove is improving; his bat (.294) is fine, thank you.

In recent seasons, the Twins have made a strong commitment to youth. It's time for the youngsters to start producing.

STAT LEADERS — 1990

BATTING
Average: Puckett, .298
Runs: Puckett, 82
Hits: Puckett, 164
Doubles: Harper, 42
Triples: Liriano, 9
Home runs: Hrbek, 22
RBIs: Gaetti, 85
Stolen bases: Gladden, 25

PITCHING
Wins: Tapani, 12
Losses: Anderson, 18
Complete games:
 Anderson, 5
Shutouts: Four with 1
Saves: Aguilera, 32
Walks: West, 78
Strikeouts: Tapani,
 Guthrie, 101

AL West
KANSAS CITY ROYALS
1990 Finish: Sixth
1991 Prediction: Seventh

Jeff Montgomery   **George Brett**

One of 1990's major disappointments, the Kansas City Royals may have found a new home near the bottom of the AL West. Unless the injury-riddled pitching staff bounces back, the club is ready for some serious rebuilding. That could eliminate them from pennant contention for years.

Certainly, the rediscovery of 1B George Brett's hitting stroke, which produced a batting title for the '90s, was a huge plus last season. At age 38 (this May), there's no telling if that was George's unofficial farewell. The Royals have already said farewell to longtime stars Frank White and Willie Wilson, so the housecleaning has begun.

Without White, 2B becomes a question mark for the first time in two decades. If Kevin Seitzer (.275) moves over, who'll play

3B? (Perhaps rookie Sean Berry.) Manager John Wathan would rather not open with Bill Pecota (.242) at second. Kurt Stillwell (.249) is steady at SS. Jeff Conine may win a spot.

Danny Tartabull (.268) missed half of '90 with torn muscles. The Royals need his power in the lineup every day. Powerful Bo Jackson (.272, 28 homers, 78 RBIs), who missed time with a shoulder injury, and Jim Eisenreich (.280) are keys to the outfield. Ex-Dodger Kirk Gibson (.260) will help. Mike Macfarlane (.255) became Kaycee's top catcher in '90 and figures to hang on for a while, with possible help from Brent Mayne.

But pitching is the key. Storm Davis can't go 7–10 again. Bret Saberhagen can't be 5–9, if he can pitch at all. Hard-throwing Tom Gordon must do better than 12–11. Ex-Red Sox Mike Boddicker (17–8) helps plenty. Bullpen chief Jeff Montgomery can repeat his 6–5, 24-save performance, but Kaycee needs an improved Mark Davis (2–7, 5.11).

STAT LEADERS — 1990

BATTING
Average: Brett, .329*
Runs: Seitzer, 91
Hits: Brett, 179
Doubles: Brett, 45**
Triples: Brett, Eisenreich, 7
Home runs: Jackson, 28
RBIs: Brett, 87
Stolen bases: Wilson, 24

PITCHING
Wins: Farr, 13
Losses: Gordon, 11
Complete games:
    Gordon, 6
Shutouts: Appier, 3
Saves: Montgomery, 24
Walks: Gordon, 99
Strikeouts: Gordon, 175

*Led league.
**Tied for league lead.

Fire-balling right-hander Ramon Martinez tries to repeat his spectacular 20–6, 2.92-ERA, 223-strikeout season for the Dodgers.

National
League
TEAM PREVIEWS

NL East
CHICAGO CUBS
1990 Finish: Fourth (tied)
1991 Prediction: First

Mike Harkey   **Shawon Dunston**

If manager Don Zimmer can find some arms (in addition to ex-Red Danny Jackson), the Cubs could be right back in the NL East pennant hunt in 1991.

Chicago's eight-man lineup is one of baseball's best. Start with 2B Ryne Sandberg (.306, 40 league-leading homers, 100 RBIs), simply baseball's best second sacker. RF Andre Dawson (.310, 27 homers, 100 RBIs) still frightens NL pitchers. 1B Mark Grace (.309, 82 RBIs) is maybe a hair behind his two super teammates. Ex-Blue Jay George Bell is a powerful addition, if his head is on straight and his defense doesn't erase his offense.

Though SS Shawon Dunston (.262) still disappoints at-bat, he holds up the left side of the infield with that gun hanging down from his right shoulder, though third base remains a problem.

Last year's LF Dwight Smith (.262) seems to be a bust, though young Derrick May (good hit, no power) is ready for the big leagues. Behind the plate, there's a pair of talented Cubbies, but either Damon Berryhill (.189 after missing much of '90 with injuries) or Joe Girardi (.270) could be dealt for more pitching.

Ah, pitching! Zimmer believes that injuries to Shawn Boskie (5–6) and Mike Harkey (12–6) destroyed the Cubs' '90 season. If he's right, the Cubs can take it all this year. But righty Greg Maddux (15–15) is streaky, righty Rick Sutcliffe (0–2) is questionable, and Mike Bielecki (8–11) and Les Lancaster (9–5) must regain their 1989 championship form. Lefty Steve Wilson (4–9) is shaky, lefty Lance Dickson may not be ready, and closer Mitch Williams (1–8) may have lost it all. Reliever Paul Assenmacher (7–2) needs help.

STAT LEADERS — 1990

BATTING
Average: Dawson, .310
Runs: Sandberg, 116*
Hits: Sandberg, 188
Doubles: Grace, 32
Triples: Dunston, 8
Home runs: Sandberg, 40*
RBIs: Sandberg, Dawson, 100
Stolen bases: Sandberg, Dunston, 25

PITCHING
Wins: Maddux, 15
Losses: Maddux, 15
Complete games: Maddux, 8
Shutouts: Maddux, 2
Saves: Williams, 16
Walks: Maddux, 71
Strikeouts: Maddux, 144

*Led league.

NL East
NEW YORK METS
1990 Finish: Second
1991 Prediction: Second

Frank Viola   **Dave Magadan**

The 1990 New York Mets were the surprise team of the NL East. The surprise? They didn't win. Now, with Darryl Strawberry off to L.A., Kevin Elster's shoulder uncertain, and most of the machine parts of the '86 world champs gone, Met losses no longer shock anyone.

Oh, the pitching is still there. The Mets' one-two punch (20–12 Frank Viola and 19–7 Doc Gooden, a possible '91 free agent) is the scariest in the majors, and righty David Cone (14–10) was the big leagues' strikeout king (233). The bullpen is in solid shape with NL save leader John Franco (5–3, 33 saves), though the Brooklyn native struggled last September. Middle relief is weak. (Julio Valera might become the key man.) And the rest of the starters (7–9 Ron Darling, unhittable but 9–14 Sid Fernandez) are no longer overpowering.

The Mets' outfield should undergo drastic changes. Speedy ex-Card Vince Coleman moves into LF. Disappointing Kevin McReynolds (.269, 24 homers) could play anywhere, but will likely move to center. Ex-Dodger Hubie Brooks (.266, 91 RBIs) will replace Straw in RF. Darryl Boston (.273), who was a pleasant '90 pickup, and Mark Carreon will back up.

1B Dave Magadan (.328) just missed an NL bat title and won an everyday job. 3B Gregg Jefferies (.283, 40 NL-leading doubles) must improve his defense. No problem with SS Howard Johnson (.244, 23 HRs, 90 RBIs, 34 steals), especially if his shoulder is healthy. SS Kevin Elster remains a question mark for 1991 (shoulder), as does fading 2B Tommy Herr.

The new catching platoon, Mackey Sasser (.307) and Charlie O'Brien, is solid, with young Todd Hundley a year away.

STAT LEADERS — 1990

BATTING
Average: Magadan, .328
Runs: Jefferies, 92
Hits: Jefferies, 171
Doubles; Jefferies, 40*
Triples: Magadan, 6
Home runs: Strawberry, 37
RBIs: Strawberry, 108
Stolen bases: Johnson, 34

PITCHING
Wins: Viola, 20
Losses: Fernandez, 14
Complete games:
   Viola, 7
Shutouts: Viola, 3
Saves: Franco, 33*
Walks: Gooden, 70
Strikeouts: Cone, 233*

*Led league.

NL East
PITTSBURGH PIRATES
1990 Finish: First
1991 Prediction: Third

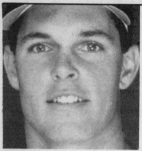

Jay Bell   **Andy Van Slyke**

The Pirates' red-hot bats, which produced a shocking 1990 NL East pennant, had
barely been tucked away when the Bucs'
1991 chances began heading south.

There isn't a better outfield in baseball
than Pittsburgh's NL MVP Barry Bonds (.301,
33 homers, 114 RBIs, 52 steals), Bobby Bonilla (.280, 32 homers, 120 RBIs), and Andy
Van Slyke (.284, 77 RBIs). But when backup
OF R.J. Reynolds (.288) split for Japan and
1B Sid Bream bolted to Atlanta last winter,
both Bonds and Bonilla screamed "cheap"
and made threats to leave after '91.

Cy Young-winner Doug Drabek (22–6, 2.76)
was overpowering a year ago and should
continue. (How did the Yankees ever let this
guy go?) His late-season partner, Zane
Smith (6–2, 1.30 ERA in 10 starts), another

free agent, re-signed with Pittsburgh.

Behind that pair, there isn't great depth on the staff, though Neal Heaton (12–9), John Smiley (9–10), and Bob Walk (7–5) aren't shabby. How long Pittsburgh can maintain a bullpen-by-committee, with closers Bill Landrum (13 saves) and Stan Belinda (8 saves), remains to be seen.

Re-signing free agents became a key to the Bucs' off-season plans. There will be changes at 1B, with Gary Redus (.247) and Carmelo Martinez high on the list. There's nothing wrong with 2B Jose Lind, SS Jay Bell (.254), or 3Bs Jeff King (.245) and free-agent Wally Backman (.292).

Off another (annual?) knee surgery, Mike LaValliere (.258) leads the catching corps, along with surprising Don Slaught (.300). There's absolutely no help available in the Bucs' farm sytem, so president Carl Barger and GM Larry Doughty will have to keep the players they have — and, somehow, keep them happy.

STAT LEADERS — 1990

BATTING
Average: Bonds, .301
Runs: Bonilla, 112
Hits: Bonilla, 175
Doubles: Bonilla, 39
Triples: Bonilla, 7
Home runs: Bonds, 33
RBIs: Bonilla, 120
Stolen bases: Bonds, 52

PITCHING
Wins: Drabek, 22*
Losses: Smiley, 10
Complete games:
   Drabek, 9
Shutouts: Drabek, 3
Saves: Landrum, 13
Walks: Drabek, 56
Strikeouts: Drabek, 131

*Led league.

PHILADELPHIA PHILLIES
1990 Finish: Fourth (tied)
1991 Prediction: Fourth

Len Dykstra   **Terry Mulholland**

The Phillie Phanatic is major-league baseball's No. 1 mascot. Unfortunately, he's the only Phillie who leads the league in anything.

True, the '90 Phils won more games than the '89 group and leapt (well, crawled) out of the NL East cellar for the first time in years. But this club is still several years (and even more players) away from a serious pennant challenge.

Manager Nick Leyva got some pleasant news when C Darren Daulton (.268, 12 homers, 57 RBIs) re-upped with the Phillies. The outfield is in solid shape, led by CF Lenny Dykstra (.325, 60 RBIs, 33 steals), the NL's leading hitter for much of '90. RF Dale Murphy (.245, but .266 with Philly) did well after his trade from Atlanta, but age is a factor. Ron Jones, returning from knee surgery, and young Wes Chamberlain could help, along with CF Sil Campusano, who's ready for bigger things.

Von Hayes (.261, 73 RBIs) remains Philly's most tradable player. SS Dickie Thon (.255) continues an amazing comeback. Mickey Morandini (.241) gets a full shot at second. Versatile Charlie Hayes (.258) makes no one forget Mike Schmidt.

Leyva has good, young starting pitching, led by Pat Combs (10–10), Terry "No-Hit" Mulholland (9–10), Jason Grimsley (3–2), and Jose DeJesus (7–8). None seems equipped to become a top, No. 1 starter. Ken Howell (8–7) returns from injury; Bruce Ruffin (6–13) suffered an off-season shoulder separation.

The bullpen is thin. Closer Roger McDowell (6–8, 22 saves) is not Randy Myers.

There are possibilities in Philadelphia, but the team still has more cracks than the town's famous big bell.

STAT LEADERS — 1990

BATTING
Average: Dykstra, .325
Runs: Dykstra, 106
Hits: Dykstra, 192*
Doubles: Dykstra, 35
Triples: Kruk, 8
Home runs: Hayes, 17
RBIs: Hayes, 73
Stolen bases: Dykstra, 33

PITCHING
Wins: Combs, 10
Losses: Ruffin, 13
Complete games:
  Mulholland, 6
Shutouts: Combs, 2
Saves: McDowell, 22
Walks: Combs, 86
Strikeouts: Combs, 108

*Tied for league lead.

NL East
MONTREAL EXPOS
1990 Finish: Third
1991 Prediction: Fifth

Delino DeShields

Tim Wallach

"They say that pitching wins pennants," said Expos right-hander Dennis Martinez. "Well, we always seem to have the pitching, but we never have enough offense."

Montreal manager Buck Rodgers must know that Dennis is right. Solving the problem may be just a little more difficult.

The Expos continue to build well with youth. 2B Delino DeShields (.289, 42 steals) was last year's rookie sensation on a hitting-poor club. Marquis Grissom (.257, 22 steals) and Larry Walker (.241; 19 homers, tying a Montreal rookie record) should become fixtures in the Olympic Stadium outfield for the next decade, with Moises Alou getting ready. That made LF Tim Raines available in trade to the White Sox for Ivan Calderon (.273). OF Otis Nixon stole

50 bases in '90 with only 231 at-bats.

1B Andres Galarraga (.256, 20 homers, 87 RBIs) looks for a bounce-back season, while 3B Tim Wallach (.296, 98 RBIs, 37 doubles) looks merely to match another super year. Spike Owen (.234) could return at SS, with Mike Fitzgerald (.243), off knee surgery, back for another go-round, and young 2B Wilfredo Cordero and C Greg Colbrunn waiting for a chance.

Pitching is Montreal's strong suit. The 'Spos were No. 1 in the NL in ERA last year. Even with Kevin Gross gone to L.A., the staff is young and deep, led by Martinez, flaky righty Oil Can Boyd (10–6, 2.93), Bill Sampen (12–7, 2.99), and Mark Gardner (7–9, 3.42). Chris Nabholz (6–2) came along late, along with Brian Barnes and Scott Anderson. The bullpen is loaded, with Steve Frey (8–2 as a rookie), recovered Tim Burke (3–3), and ex-White Sox Barry Jones (11–4).

This is the NL's team of the future.

STAT LEADERS — 1990

BATTING
Average: Wallach, .296
Runs: DeShields,
   Wallach, 69
Hits: Wallach, 185
Doubles: Wallach, 37
Triples: DeShields, 6
Home runs:
   Wallach, 21
RBIs: Wallach, 98
Stolen bases: Nixon, 50

PITCHING
Wins: Sampen, 12
Losses: Gross, 12
Complete games:
   De. Martinez, 7
Shutouts: Boyd, Gardner, 3
Saves: Burke, 20
Walks: Gross, 65
Strikeouts:
   De. Martinez, 156

NL East
ST. LOUIS CARDINALS
1990 Finish: Sixth
1991 Prediction: Sixth

Felix Jose   **Pedro Guerrero**

When the Cardinals finished last in the NL East in 1990, it marked the team's first cellar visit in 72 years. From the look of things, it could well happen again in 1991.

Manager Joe Torre, who has a brilliant future as a baseball broadcaster, hopes his career with a microphone is years away. It will be, if Cardinal management is patient. The Cards have speed and some young talent but no power, a questionable pitching staff, and declining defense.

Look for 1990 catching prospect Todd Zeile (.244, 57 RBIs) to open the '91 season at third base, with ex-3B Terry Pendleton (.230) now employed by the Braves. That will make Tom Pagnozzi (.277 and fine defense) the first-string catcher. The St. Louis youth movement should also produce starting roles for ex-Athletic Felix Jose (.271 in September) in right and Ray Lankford (.286 and great speed) in center. LF Bernard Gilkey (.297 in a late trial) will get a full look this spring, with Vince Coleman (.292, league-leading 77 steals) off to the Mets.

1B Pedro Guerrero (.281, 80 RBIs), St. Louis's biggest power threat, was off-season trade bait. If he's gone, look for Rod Brewer (.240 in 14 games) to take over. Versatile Jose Oquendo (.252) should return at 2B, with aging Ozzie Smith (.254) hanging on at short.

Pitching, long the Cardinal strong suit, is a strong suit no longer. On a ball club with no power and little scoring, that spells disaster. Torre looks to hard-throwing Jose DeLeon (7–19, the losingest NL pitcher), Bob Tewksbury (10–9), Bryn Smith (9–8), and highly sought lefty Joe Magrane (10–17). Hefty closer Lee Smith (3–4, 2.10, 27 saves) needs help in the bullpen.

STAT LEADERS — 1990

BATTING
Average: McGee, .335*
Runs: McGee, 76
Hits: McGee, 168
Doubles: McGee, 32
Triples: Coleman, 9
Home runs: Zeile, 15
RBIs: Guerrero, 80
Stolen bases: Coleman, 77*

*Led league.

PITCHING
Wins: Tudor, 12
Losses: DeLeon, 19*
Complete games:
   Magrane,
   Tewksbury, 3
Shutouts: Tewksbury,
   Magrane, 2
Saves: L. Smith, 27
Walks: DeLeon, 86
Strikeouts: DeLeon, 164

LOS ANGELES DODGERS
1990 Finish: Second
1991 Prediction: First

Eddie Murray   **Mike Scioscia**

With a little bit of luck, the Dodgers might have caught the Cincinnati Reds in the NL West last year. In baseball, however, you have to make your own luck. So the Dodgers went out and spent $20-million-plus on ex-Met Darryl Strawberry. The chase for the '91 flag began on that November evening.

Straw (.277, 37 homers, 108 RBIs) makes an already-powerful Dodger lineup downright scary. Darryl joins OF Kal Daniels (.296, 94 RBIs, 27 homers) and 1B Eddie Murray (.330, 95 RBIs, 26 homers) to form an absolutely awesome mid-lineup threesome.

SS Alfredo Griffin (.210) must look over his shoulder at rookie Jose Offerman (only .155 in a September trial). 3B appears to be wide open. The Dodger infield platoon of Lenny Harris (.304) and Mike Sharperson (.297) will work at 2B. Defense is a major Dodger problem, save for C Mike Scioscia (.264).

The Dodgers signed ex-Giant Brett Butler (.309, 51 steals) to replace Kirk Gibson in CF. A great leadoff hitter, Butler will be an outstanding table-setter for Daniels, Murray, and Strawberry.

The starting mound staff may well be the NL's best, led by young righty Ramon Martinez (20–6, 2.92, league-leading 12 complete games), Mike Morgan (11–15, 3.75), and ex-Expo Kevin Gross (9–12). If Orel Hershiser (only four games in '90) and Tim Belcher (missed three months) return healthy, the Dodgers will be loaded, even though one-time hero Fernando Valenzuela (13–13) is probably gone. Ex-Met Bob Ojeda could start or relieve. Reliever Jay Howell (5–5, 16 saves) needs help.

Youngsters like Danny Opperman, Jaime McAndrew, Kiki Jones, and Jason Brosnan are on their way, but probably not before '92.

STAT LEADERS — 1990

BATTING
Average: Murray, .330
Runs: Murray, 96
Hits: Murray, 184
Doubles: Brooks, 28
Triples: Javier, Harris, 4
Home runs: Daniels, 27
RBIs: Murray, 95
Stolen bases: Samuel, 38

PITCHING
Wins: Martinez, 20
Losses: Morgan, 15
Complete games:
   Martinez, 12*
Shutouts: Morgan, 4**
Saves: Howell, 16
Walks: Valenzuela, 77
Strikeouts: Martinez, 223

*Led league.
**Tied for league lead.

NL West
SAN FRANCISCO GIANTS
1990 Finish: Third
1991 Prediction: Second

Jeff Brantley

Kevin Mitchell

If San Francisco can find the pitching to go with its power and defense, the Giants will be right back in the NL West hunt. No one in baseball enjoys the punch the Candlestick gang does from the 3–4–5 slots in the batting order. But unless the pitchers find some way to hold the opponents, even a repeat of the team's third-place finish in '90 may be too much to ask for.

The Giants committed $10-million to pick up lefty Bud Black, who had been with Toronto for about three weeks. He'll help, but perhaps not enough. Can San Fran continue to count on chubby Rick Reuschel (3–6, 3.93), Don Robinson (10–7, 4.57), or Mike LaCoss (6–4, 3.94)? Will Kelly Downs (3–2, 3.43 in nine starts) stay healthy all year? John Burkett (14–7, 3.79) became the ace of the staff in '90, after starting the year in the minors. He and Trevor Wilson (8–7, 4.00) should get even better in '91. Jeff Brantley (5–3, 1.56, 19 saves) and ex-Yankee ace closer Dave Righetti will man the bullpen until Mark Dewey is ready.

That middle-of-the-order power — 1B Will Clark (2.95, 19 homers, 95 RBIs), LF Kevin Mitchell (.290, 35 homers, 93 RBIs), and 3B Matt Williams (.277, 33 homers, 122 league-leading RBIs) — is without equal, even in a year when Clark and Mitchell slip a hair. Williams is becoming the game's best 3B.

SS Jose Uribe is trade bait, with youngsters like Mike Benjamin and Andres Santana on the way. CF Brett Butler (.309, 51 steals) is gone, with ex-Card/Athletic CF Willie McGee (an NL-leading .335) stepping in and joining RF Kevin Bass. 2B Robby Thompson (.245) is first-rate.

C Terry Kennedy (.277) will hold on, waiting till Steve Decker is ready.

STAT LEADERS — 1990

BATTING
Average: Butler, .309
Runs: Butler, 108
Hits: Butler, 192
Doubles: Williams, 27
Triples: Butler, 9
Home runs: Mitchell, 35
RBIs: Williams, 122*
Stolen bases: Butler, 51

*Led league.

PITCHING
Wins: Burkett, 14
Losses: Garrelts, 11
Complete games: Garrelts, Robinson, 4
Shutouts: Garrelts, Wilson, 2
Saves: Brantley, 19
Walks, Garrelts, 70
Strikeouts: Burkett, 118

NL West
CINCINNATI REDS
1990 Finish: First
1991 Prediction: Third

Tom Browning

Jose Rijo

The surprise World Series sweepers should be in the thick of things again in '91, if owner Marge Schott is willing to part with a few bucks. Marge, who throws money around like other folks toss boulders, faced the off-season with a bunch of free agents and salary-arbitration cases. The outcome will set the tone for Cincy for years.

The returning cast, if happy, is awesome. Even without free-agent Danny Jackson (to Cubs), the pitching is topflight. Tom Browning (15–9) re-upped with Cincinnati, rejoining World Series MVP Jose Rijo (14–8), Jack Armstrong (12–9), and Scott Scudder (5–5). Rick Mahler (7–6) may be in trouble. The bullpen, led by super-closer Randall Myers (4–6, 2.08, 31 saves), Rob Dibble (8–3, 1.74, 11 saves), and sometime starter Norm

Charlton (12–9), is the best in the business.

1B Hal Morris (.340) has made Todd Benzinger (.253) available for trade, with Terry Lee arriving this year and Reggie Jefferson ready for 1992 delivery. 2B Mariano Duncan (.306), another World Series hero, joins super SS Barry Larkin (.301) in one of the game's best DP combos. 3B Chris Sabo (.270, 25 homers) continues to improve in every department.

If LF Eric Davis (.260, 24 homers, 86 RBIs) is healthy and forgets his ambulance-plane argument of last October (spend the money, Marge!), he's as good as anyone. CF Billy Hatcher (.276) and RF Paul O'Neill (.270, but only 16 homers) complete the outfield trio. O'Neill is the key to improved Reds power, their only shortcoming. C Joe Oliver (.231) is adequate behind the plate.

The Reds might not repeat, but the tools to get it done are in place. Now the ball is in Marge's court.

STAT LEADERS — 1990

BATTING
Average: Duncan, .306
Runs: Sabo, 95
Hits: Larkin, 185
Doubles: Sabo, 38
Triples: Duncan, 11*
Home runs: Sabo, 25
RBIs: Davis, 86
Stolen bases: Larkin, Hatcher, 30

PITCHING
Wins: Browning, 15
Losses: Three with 9
Complete games: Rijo, 7
Shutouts: Five with 1
Saves: Myers, 31
Walks: Rijo, 78
Strikeouts: Rijo, 152

*Led league.

NL West
SAN DIEGO PADRES
1990 Finish: Fourth (tied)
1991 Prediction: Fourth

Ed Whitson

Fred McGriff

When the 1990 season began, the Padres, under manager-GM Jack McKeon, were considered a contender for the NL West pennant. By the time it ended, All-Star RF Tony Gwynn wasn't talking to his teammates, McKeon was gone, and so were the Padres.

It's hard to figure. San Diego has tons of potential, but that's been it. Potential. 1B Jack Clark (.266, 25 homers), a frequent troublemaker, could have much bigger years — but they'll be in Boston. Ex-Blue Jay 1B Fred McGriff moves right in. If 2B Paul Faries is ready to step in, he'll pair up with ex-Blue Jay SS Tony Fernandez, the AL's best. 3B Mike Pagliarulo (.254) will be replaced by Faries, Bip Roberts, or ex-Ranger Scott Coolbaugh.

Gwynn (.309) is still among baseball's best hitters. With Joe Carter gone to Toronto in the McGriff-Fernandez trade, look for Thomas Howard or Gerald Clark in LF, with Shawn Abner or Darrin Jackson in CF.

Behind the plate, Benito Santiago (.270) is the National League's (maybe baseball's) best.

If Padre starters can get a lead to the bullpen, they have a shot. Righty Greg Harris (8–8, 2.30) and lefty Craig Lefferts 7–5, 23 saves) form a mighty duo. But the starters leave much to be desired, with Eric Show (6–8) and Dennis Rasmussen (11–15) probably headed out of town. Lefty Bruce Hurst (11–9) leads the returnees, with right-handers Andy Benes (10–11) and Ed Whitson (14–9, 2.60) set in the rotation.

Manager Greg Riddoch, who took over from McKeon at midseason in '90, looks for help from rookie Dave Staton and pitcher Rafael Valdez.

STAT LEADERS — 1990

BATTING
Average: Gwynn, Roberts, .309
Runs: Roberts, 104
Hits: Gwynn, 177
Doubles: Roberts, 36
Triples: Gwynn, 10
Home runs: Clark, 25
RBIs: Carter, 115
Stolen bases: Roberts, 46

PITCHING
Wins: Whitson, 14
Losses: Rasmussen, 15
Complete games: Hurst, 9
Shutouts: Hurst, 4*
Saves: Lefferts, 23
Walks: Benes, 69
Strikeouts: Hurst, 162

*Tied for league lead.

NL West
ATLANTA BRAVES
1990 Finish: Sixth
1991 Prediction: Fifth

Tom Glavine   **Lonnie Smith**

And the beat goes on. The Braves, who targeted .500 as their goal for 1990, will be pleased if they can just get out of the NL West cellar. It won't be easy.

The foundation for improvement is weak, though not totally absent. There's plenty of power, some of it due to the short fences at Atlanta Stadium. The Braves were second in the NL in homers, led by surprising OF Ron Gant's 32. Top NL rookie RF Dave Justice pitched in with another 28. Starting pitchers John Smoltz (14–11) and Tom Glavine (10–12) are future All-Stars, though one may have to be dealt for offense and, especially, defense.

That's the start of some good things. There isn't that much more. Ex-Pirate 1B Sid Bream replaces Nick Esasky, whose vertigo has not been cured. SS Andres Thomas (.219) may need a change of scenery, which would open spots up the middle for Jeff Treadway (.283) and Jeff Blauser (.269). Defense at 3B should be improved with the addition of ex-Card Terry Pendleton (.230). 3B Jim Presley (.242) is a free agent. And LF Lonnie Smith (.305), whose shabby glove outweighs his big bat, may be gone.

If Smoltz and Glavine are still around, they'll be joined by lefty Steve Avery (3–11) and righty Paul Marak (1–2 late). The bullpen, a disaster in '90, shows promise, particularly if closer Mike Stanton returns healthy. Otherwise, it's righty Jeff Parrett and lefty Kent Mercker and serious prayer.

Catcher Greg Olson, who barely made the club last spring, wound up on the All-Star team. Actually, there's decent depth behind the plate where Jimmy Kremers and Kelly Mann are ready to step in with the parent club. But until the Braves develop speed, defense, and pitching, they seem doomed.

STAT LEADERS — 1990

BATTING
Average: Smith, .305
Runs: Gant, 107
Hits: Gant, 174
Doubles: Gant, Presley, 34
Triples: Smith, 9
Home runs: Gant, 32
RBIs: Gant, 84
Stolen bases: Gant, 33

*Led league.

PITCHING
Wins: Smoltz, 14
Losses: Glavine, 12
Complete games:
  Smoltz, 6
Shutouts: Smoltz,
  Leibrandt, 2
Saves: Mercker, 7
Walks: Smoltz, 90*
Strikeouts: Smoltz, 170

NL West
HOUSTON ASTROS
1990 Finish: Fourth (tied)
1991 Prediction: Sixth

Mark Portugal

Craig Biggio

After hanging around the top of the NL West from 1986–89, the Astros slipped badly in 1990. The slippage will likely continue, until the team's fine young minor-league talent is ready for the big time.

It's not that the current crew is entirely without hope. There are some excellent arms on the pitching staff and good team speed. But the 'Stros don't hit for power, don't score many runs, and don't play solid defense. On balance, that's not a healthy outlook. The trading of Bill Doran, Larry Andersen, and Dan Schatzeder late last season heralded a rebuildilng process that will continue.

On the plus side, there's OF/SS Eric Yelding (.254, 64 steals), the speed king. 1B Glenn Davis (.251, 64 RBIs, 22 homers, despite missing nine weeks with a rib-cage injury) should be back, but 1B-OF Franklin Stubbs (.261, 71 RBIs, 23 homers) hit the road for Milwaukee. 3B Ken Caminiti (.242) could give way to ex-Red Sox farmhand Jeff Bagwell. Andy Mota could start at 2B. OF Eric Anthony (.192) remains a project. But the future leader is Craig Biggio (.276, 42 RBIs, 25 stolen bases), who must find a position, any position.

Young Karl Rhodes could be the '91 left fielder. Weak-gloved Andujar Cedeno could be the SS by mid-'91. IF Luis Gonzalez could provide power — eventually.

On the mound, lefty Jim Deshaies (7–12) needs more help. Righty Mark Portugal (11–10) should continue to improve, while ex-superstar Mike Scott (9–13, 3.81) faded badly in '90. The Astros will need to find a new closer because free-agent Dave Smith (6–6, 23 saves) signed with the Cubs. Righties Randy Hennis, Darryl Kile, and Jeff Juden could join lefty relievers Brian Meyer and Al Osuna on the roster.

STAT LEADERS — 1990

BATTING
Average: Biggio, .276
Runs: Yelding, 69
Hits: Biggio, 153
Doubles: Biggio, 24
Triples: Candaele, 6
Home runs: Stubbs, 23
RBIs: Stubbs, 71
Stolen bases: Yelding, 64

PITCHING
Wins: Darwin,
   Portugal, 11
Losses: Gullickson, 14
Complete games: Scott, 4
Shutouts: Scott, 2
Saves: Smith, 23
Walks: Deshaies, 84
Strikeouts: Portugal, 136

As the Texas Rangers battle for the lead in
the AL West, hard-hitting Rafael Palmeiro
(.319) will set the pace.

1990
STATISTICS

AMERICAN LEAGUE
Batting

(35 or more at-bats)
*Bats Left-Handed   †Switch-Hitter

Batter and Team	AVG	G	AB	R	H	HR	RBI	SB
Alomar, S., Cle.	.290	132	445	60	129	9	66	4
Anderson, B., Bal.*	.231	89	234	24	54	3	24	15
Anderson, K., Cal.	.308	49	143	16	44	1	5	0
Azocar, O., NY*	.248	65	214	18	53	5	19	7
Baerga, C., Cle.†	.260	108	312	46	81	7	47	0
Baines, H., Tex.-Oak.*	.284	135	415	52	118	16	65	0
Balboni, S., N.Y.	.192	116	266	24	51	17	34	0
Barfield, J., N.Y.	.246	153	476	69	117	25	78	4
Barrett, M., Bos.	.226	62	159	15	36	0	13	4
Bell, G., Tor.	.265	142	562	67	149	21	86	3
Bergman, D., Det.*	.278	100	205	21	57	2	26	3
Bichette, D., Cal.	.255	109	349	40	89	15	53	5
Blankenship, L., Oak.	.191	86	136	18	26	0	10	3
Blowers, M., N.Y.	.188	48	144	16	27	5	21	1
Boggs, W., Bos.*	.302	155	619	89	187	6	63	0
Boone, B., K.C.	.239	40	117	11	28	0	9	1
Borders, P., Tor.	.286	125	346	36	99	15	49	0
Bradley, P., Bal.-Chi.	.256	117	422	59	108	4	31	17
Bradley, S., Sea.*	.223	101	233	11	52	1	28	0
Braggs, G., Mil.	.248	37	113	17	28	3	13	5
Brett, G., K.C.*	.329	142	544	82	179	14	87	9
Briley, G., Sea.*	.246	125	337	40	83	5	29	16
Brock, G., Mil.*	.248	123	367	42	91	7	50	4
Brookens, T., Cle.	.266	64	154	18	41	1	20	0
Browne, J., Cle.†	.267	140	513	92	137	6	50	12
Brumley, M., Sea.†	.224	62	147	19	33	0	7	2
Brunansky, T., Bos.	.267	129	461	61	123	15	71	5
Buckner, B., Bos.*	.186	22	43	4	8	1	3	0
Buechele, S., Tex.	.215	91	251	30	54	7	30	1
Buhner, J., Sea.	.276	51	163	16	45	7	33	2
Burks, E., Bos.	.296	152	588	89	174	21	89	9

Batter and Team	AVG	G	AB	R	H	HR	RBI	SB
Bush, R., Min.*	.243	73	181	17	44	6	18	0
Calderon, I., Chi.	.273	158	607	85	166	14	74	32
Canseco, J., Oak.	.274	131	481	83	132	37	101	19
Castillo, C., Min.	.219	64	137	11	30	0	12	0
Cerone, R., N.Y.	.302	49	139	12	42	2	11	0
Coachman, P., Cal.	.311	16	45	3	14	0	5	0
Cole, A., Cle.*	.300	63	227	43	68	0	13	40
Coles, D., Sea.-Det.	.209	89	215	22	45	3	20	0
Coolbaugh, S., Tex.	.200	67	180	21	36	2	13	1
Cotto, H., Sea.	.259	127	355	40	92	4	33	21
Cuyler, M., Det.†	.255	19	51	8	13	0	8	1
Daugherty, J., Tex.†	.300	125	310	36	93	6	47	0
Davis, A., Sea.*	.283	140	494	63	140	17	68	0
Davis, C., Cal.†	.265	113	412	58	109	12	58	1
Deer, R., Mil.	.209	134	440	57	92	27	69	2
Devereaux, M., Bal.	.240	108	367	48	88	12	49	13
Diaz, E., Mil.	.271	86	218	27	59	0	14	3
Disarcina, G., Cal.	.140	18	57	8	8	0	0	1
Dorsett, B., N.Y.	.143	14	35	2	5	0	0	0
Downing, B., Cal.	.273	96	330	47	90	14	51	0
Ducey, R., Tor.*	.302	19	53	7	16	0	7	1
Dwyer, J., Min.*	.190	37	63	7	12	1	5	0
Eisenreich, J., K.C.*	.280	142	496	61	139	5	51	12
Espinoza, A., N.Y.	.224	150	438	31	98	2	20	1
Espy, C., Tex.†	.127	52	71	10	9	0	1	11
Evans, D., Bos.	.249	123	445	66	111	13	63	3
Felder, M., Mil.†	.274	121	237	38	65	3	27	20
Felix, J., Tor.†	.263	127	463	73	122	15	65	13
Fermin, F., Cle.	.256	148	414	47	106	1	40	3
Fernandez, T., Tor.†	.276	161	635	84	175	4	66	26
Fielder, C., Det.	.277	159	573	104	159	51	132	0
Finley, S., Bal.*	.256	142	464	46	119	3	37	22
Fisk, C., Chi.	.285	137	452	65	129	18	65	7
Fletcher, S., Chi.	.242	151	509	54	123	4	56	1
Franco, J., Tex.	.296	157	582	96	172	11	69	31
Fryman, T., Det.	.297	66	232	32	69	9	27	3
Gaetti, G., Min.	.229	154	577	61	132	16	85	6

Batter and Team	AVG	G	AB	R	H	HR	RBI	SB
Gagne, G., Min.	.235	138	388	38	91	7	38	8
Gallagher, D., Chi.-Bal.	.254	68	126	12	32	0	7	1
Gallego, M., Oak.	.206	140	389	36	80	3	34	5
Gantner, J., Mil.*	.263	88	323	36	85	0	25	18
Geren, R., N.Y.	.213	110	277	21	59	8	31	0
Giles, B., Sea.	.232	45	95	15	22	4	11	2
Gladden, D., Min.	.275	136	534	64	147	5	40	25
Gomez, L., Bal.	.231	12	39	3	9	0	1	0
Gonzales, R., Bal.	.214	67	103	13	22	1	12	1
Gonzalez, J., Tex.	.289	25	90	11	26	4	12	0
Grebeck, C., Chi.	.168	59	119	7	20	1	9	0
Green, G., Tex.	.216	62	88	10	19	0	8	1
Greenwell, M., Bos.*	.297	159	610	71	181	14	73	8
Griffey Jr., K., Sea.*	.300	155	597	91	179	22	80	16
Griffey Sr., K., Sea.*	.377	21	77	13	29	3	18	0
Gruber, K., Tor.	.274	150	592	92	162	31	118	14
Guillen, O., Chi.	.279	160	516	61	144	1	58	13
Hall, M., N.Y.*	.258	113	360	41	93	12	46	0
Hamilton, D., Mil.*	.295	89	156	27	46	1	18	10
Harper, B., Min.	.294	134	479	61	141	6	54	3
Hassey, R., Oak.*	.213	94	254	18	54	5	22	0
Heath, M., Det.	.270	122	370	46	100	7	38	7
Heep, D., Bos.*	.174	41	69	3	12	0	8	0
Henderson, D., Oak.	.271	127	450	65	122	20	63	3
Henderson, R., Oak.	.325	136	489	119	159	28	61	65
Hernandez, K., Cle.*	.200	43	130	7	26	1	8	0
Hill, D., Cal.†	.264	103	352	36	93	3	32	1
Hill, G., Tor.	.231	84	260	47	60	12	32	8
Hoiles, C., Bal.	.190	23	63	7	12	1	6	0
Horn, S., Bal.*	.248	79	246	30	61	14	45	0
Howard, S., Oak.	.231	21	52	5	12	0	1	0
Howell, J., Cal.*	.228	105	316	35	72	8	33	3
Hrbek, K., Min.*	.287	143	492	61	141	22	79	5
Hulett, T., Bal.	.255	53	153	16	39	3	16	1
Huson, J., Tex.*	.240	145	396	57	95	0	28	12
Incaviglia, P., Tex.	.233	153	529	59	123	24	85	3
Jackson, B., K.C.	.272	111	405	74	110	28	78	15

Batter and Team	AVG	G	AB	R	H	HR	RBI	SB
Jacoby, B., Cle.	.293	155	553	77	162	14	75	1
James, C., Cle.	.299	140	528	62	158	12	70	4
James, D., Cle.*	.274	87	248	28	68	1	22	5
Jefferson, S., Bal.-Cle.† ...	.231	59	117	22	27	2	10	9
Jeltz, S., K.C.†	.155	74	103	11	16	0	10	1
Jennings, J., Oak.*	.192	64	156	19	30	2	14	0
Johnson, L., Chi.*	.285	151	541	76	154	1	51	36
Jones, T., Det.-Sea.	.260	75	204	23	53	6	24	1
Jose, F., Oak.†	.264	101	341	42	90	8	39	8
Joyner, W., Cal.*	.268	83	310	35	83	8	41	2
Karkovice, R., Chi.	.246	68	183	30	45	6	20	2
Kelly, R., N.Y.	.285	162	641	85	183	15	61	42
Kittle, R., Chi.-Bal.	.231	105	338	33	78	18	46	0
Komminsk, B., Bal.	.238	46	101	18	24	3	8	1
Kunkel, J., Tex.	.170	99	200	17	34	3	17	2
Kutcher, R., Bos.	.230	63	74	18	17	1	5	3
Lansford, C., Oak.	.268	134	507	58	136	3	50	16
Larkin, G., Min.†	.269	119	401	46	108	5	42	5
Lee, M., Tor.†	.243	117	391	45	95	6	41	3
Lemon, C., Det.	.258	104	322	39	83	5	32	3
Leonard, J., Sea.	.251	134	478	39	120	10	75	4
Lewis, D., Oak.	.229	25	35	4	8	0	1	2
Leyritz, J., N.Y.	.257	92	303	28	78	5	25	2
Liriano, N., Tor.-Min.†	.234	103	355	46	83	1	28	8
Lusader, S., Det.*	.241	45	87	13	21	2	16	0
Lyons, S., Chi.*	.192	94	146	22	28	1	11	1
Mass, K., N.Y.*	.252	79	254	42	64	21	41	1
Macfarlane, M., K.C.	.255	124	400	37	102	6	58	1
Mack, S., Min.	.326	125	313	50	102	8	44	13
Maldonado, C., Cle.	.273	155	590	76	161	22	95	3
Manrique, F., Min.	.237	69	228	22	54	5	29	2
Manto, J., Cle.	.224	30	76	12	17	2	14	0
Marshall, M., Bos.	.286	30	112	10	32	4	12	0
Martinez, C., Chi.	.224	92	272	18	61	4	24	0
Martinez, E., Sea.	.302	144	487	71	147	11	49	1
Martinez, T., Sea.*	.221	24	68	4	15	0	5	0
Marzano, J., Bos.	.241	32	83	8	20	0	6	0

Batter and Team	AVG	G	AB	R	H	HR	RBI	SB
Mattingly, D., N.Y.*	.256	102	394	40	101	5	42	1
McGee, W., Oak.†	.274	29	113	23	31	0	15	3
McGriff, F., Tor.*	.300	153	557	91	167	35	88	5
McGwire, M., Oak.	.235	156	523	87	123	39	108	2
McKnight, J., Bal.†	.200	29	75	11	15	1	4	0
McLemore, M., Cal.-Cle.†	.150	28	60	6	9	0	2	1
McRae, B., K.C.†	.286	46	168	21	48	2	23	4
Melvin, B., Bal.	.243	93	301	30	73	5	37	0
Meulens, H., N.Y.	.241	23	83	12	20	3	10	1
Milligan, R., Bal.	.265	109	362	64	96	20	60	6
Molitor, P., Mil.	.285	103	418	64	119	12	45	18
Morman, R., K.C.	.270	12	37	5	10	1	3	0
Moseby, L., Det.*	.248	122	431	64	107	14	51	17
Moses, J., Min.†	.221	115	172	26	38	1	14	2
Mulliniks, R., Tor.*	.289	57	97	11	28	2	16	2
Munoz, P., Min.	.271	22	85	13	23	0	5	3
Myers, G., Tor.*	.236	87	250	33	59	5	22	0
Naehring, T., Bos.	.271	24	85	10	23	2	12	0
Newman, A., Min.†	.242	144	388	43	94	0	30	13
Nokes, M., Det.-N.Y.*	.248	136	351	33	87	11	40	2
O'Brien, C., Mil.	.186	46	145	11	27	0	11	0
O'Brien, P., Sea.*	.224	108	366	32	82	5	27	0
Olerud, J., Tor.*	.265	111	358	43	95	14	48	0
Orsulak, J., Bal.*	.269	124	413	49	111	11	57	6
Ortiz, J., Min.	.335	71	170	18	57	0	18	0
Orton, J., Cal.	.190	31	84	8	16	1	6	0
Palacios, R., K.C.	.232	41	56	8	13	2	9	2
Palmeiro, R., Tex.*	.319	154	598	72	191	14	89	3
Parker, D., Mil.*	.289	157	610	71	176	21	92	4
Parrish, L., Cal.	.268	133	470	54	126	24	70	2
Pasqua, D., Chi.*	.274	112	325	43	89	13	58	1
Pecota, B., K.C.	.242	87	240	43	58	5	20	8
Pena, T., Bos.	.263	143	491	62	129	7	56	8
Perry, G., K.C.*	.254	133	465	57	118	8	57	17
Petralli, G., Tex.*	.255	133	325	28	83	0	21	0
Pettis, G., Tex.†	.239	136	423	66	101	3	31	38
Phelps, K., Oak.-Cle.*	.150	56	120	10	18	1	6	1

Batter and Team	AVG	G	AB	R	H	HR	RBI	SB
Phillips, T., Det.†	.251	152	573	97	144	8	55	19
Polonia, L., N.Y.-Cal.*	.335	120	403	52	135	2	35	21
Puckett, K., Min.	.298	146	551	82	164	12	80	5
Quintana, C., Bos.	.287	149	512	56	147	7	67	1
Quirk, J., Oak.*	.281	56	121	12	34	3	26	0
Randolph, W., Oak.	.257	93	292	37	75	1	21	6
Ray, J., Cal.†	.277	105	404	47	112	5	43	2
Reed, J., Bos.	.289	155	598	70	173	5	51	4
Reimer, K., Tex.*	.260	64	100	5	26	2	15	0
Reynolds, H., Sea.†	.252	160	642	100	162	5	55	31
Ripken, B., Bal.	.291	129	406	48	118	3	38	5
Ripken, C., Bal.	.250	161	600	78	150	21	84	3
Rivera, L., Bos.	.225	118	346	38	78	7	45	4
Robidoux, B., Bos.*	.182	27	44	3	8	1	4	0
Romero, E., Det.	.229	32	70	8	16	0	4	0
Romine, K., Bos.	.272	70	136	21	37	2	14	4
Russell, J., Tex.	.273	68	128	16	35	2	8	1
Salas, M., Det.*	.232	74	164	18	38	9	24	0
Sanders, D., N.Y.*	.158	57	133	24	21	3	9	8
Sax, S., N.Y.	.260	155	615	70	160	4	42	43
Schaefer, J., Sea.	.206	55	107	11	22	0	6	4
Schofield, D., Cal.	.255	99	310	41	79	1	18	3
Schroeder, B., Cal.	.224	18	58	7	13	4	9	0
Schu, R., Cal.	.268	61	157	19	42	6	14	0
Schultz, J., K.C.*	.258	30	66	5	17	0	6	0
Segui, D., Bal.†	.244	40	123	14	30	2	15	0
Seitzer, K., K.C.	.275	158	622	91	171	6	38	7
Sheets, L., Det.*	.261	131	360	40	94	10	52	1
Sheffield, G., Mil.	.294	125	487	67	143	10	67	25
Shelby, J., Det.†	.248	78	222	22	55	4	20	3
Shumpert, T., K.C.	.275	32	91	7	25	0	8	3
Sierra, R., Tex.†	.280	159	608	70	170	16	96	9
Sinatro, M., Sea.	.300	30	50	2	15	0	4	1
Skinner, J., Cle.	.252	49	139	16	35	2	16	0
Synder, C., Cle.	.233	123	438	46	102	14	55	1
Sojo, L., Tor.	.225	33	80	14	18	1	9	1
Sorrento, P., Min.*	.207	41	121	11	25	5	13	1

Batter and Team	AVG	G	AB	R	H	HR	RBI	SB
Sosa, S., Chi.	.233	153	532	72	124	15	70	32
Spiers, B., Mil.*	.242	112	363	44	88	2	36	11
Stanley, M., Tex.	.249	103	189	21	47	2	19	1
Steinbach, T., Oak.	.251	114	379	32	95	9	57	0
Stevens, L., Cal.*	.214	67	248	28	53	7	32	1
Stillwell, K., K.C.†	.249	144	506	60	126	3	51	0
Surhoff, B., Mil.*	.276	135	474	55	131	6	59	18
Sveum, D., Mil.†	.197	48	117	15	23	1	12	0
Tabler, P., K.C.	.272	75	195	12	53	1	19	0
Tartabull, D., K.C.	.268	88	313	41	84	15	60	1
Tettleton, M., Bal.†	.223	135	444	68	99	15	51	2
Thomas, F., Chi.	.330	60	191	39	63	7	31	0
Thurman, G., K.C.	.233	23	60	5	14	0	3	1
Tolleson, W., N.Y.†	.149	73	74	12	11	0	4	1
Trammell, A., Det.	.304	146	559	71	170	14	89	12
Valle, D., Sea.	.214	107	308	37	66	7	33	1
Vaughn, G., Mil.	.220	120	382	51	84	17	61	7
Velarde, R., N.Y.	.210	95	229	21	48	5	19	0
Venable, M., Cal.*	.259	93	189	26	49	4	21	5
Ventura, R., Chi.*	.249	150	493	48	123	5	54	1
Vizquel, O., Sea.†	.247	81	255	19	63	2	18	4
Walker, G., Chi.-Bal.*	.154	16	39	2	6	0	2	1
Ward, G., Det.	.256	106	309	32	79	9	46	2
Ward., T., Cle.†	.348	14	46	10	16	1	10	3
Washington, C., Cal.-N.Y.*	.167	45	114	7	19	1	9	4
Webster, M., Cle.†	.252	128	437	58	110	12	55	22
Weiss, W., Oak.†	.265	138	445	50	118	2	35	9
Whitaker, L., Det.*	.237	132	472	75	112	18	60	8
White, D., Cal.†	.217	125	443	57	96	11	44	21
White, F., K.C.	.216	82	241	20	52	2	21	1
Whiten, M., Tor.†	.273	33	88	12	24	2	7	2
Williams, K., Det.-Tor.	.161	106	155	23	25	0	13	9
Wilson, M., Tor.†	.265	147	588	81	156	3	51	23
Wilson, W., K.C.†	.290	115	307	49	89	2	42	24
Winfield, D., N.Y.-Cal.	.267	132	475	70	127	21	78	0
Worthington, C., Bal.	.226	133	425	46	96	8	44	1
Yount, R., Mil.	.247	158	587	98	145	17	77	15

AMERICAN LEAGUE
Pitching

(80 or more innings pitched)
*Throws Left-Handed

Pitcher and Team	W	L	ERA	G	IP	H	BB	SO
Abbott, J., Cal.*	10	14	4.51	33	211.2	246	72	105
Abbott, P., Min.	0	5	5.97	7	34.2	37	28	25
Acker, J., Tor.	4	4	3.83	59	91.2	103	30	54
Aguilera, R., Min.	5	3	2.76	56	65.1	55	19	61
Anderson, A., Min.*	7	18	4.53	31	188.2	214	39	82
Appier, K., K.C.	12	8	2.76	32	185.2	179	54	127
Ballard, J., Bal.*	2	11	4.93	44	133.1	152	42	50
Berenguer, J., Min.	8	5	3.41	51	100.1	85	58	77
Black, B., Cle.-Tor.*	13	11	3.57	32	206.2	181	61	106
Blyleven, B., Cal.	8	7	5.24	23	134.0	163	25	69
Boddicker, M., Bos.	17	8	3.36	34	228.0	225	69	143
Bolton, T., Bos.*	10	5	3.38	21	119.2	111	47	65
Bosio, C., Mil.	4	9	4.00	20	132.2	131	38	76
Brown, K., Tex.	12	10	3.60	26	180.0	175	60	88
Cadaret, G., N.Y.*	5	4	4.15	54	121.1	120	64	80
Candiotti, T., Cle.	15	11	3.65	31	202.0	207	55	128
Cary, C., N.Y.*	6	2	4.19	28	156.2	155	55	134
Cerutti, J., Tor.*	9	9	4.76	30	140.0	162	49	49
Clemens, R., Bos.	21	6	1.93	31	228.1	193	54	209
Crawford, S., K.C.	5	4	4.16	46	80.0	79	23	54
Crim, C., Mil.	3	5	3.47	67	85.2	88	23	39
Davis, S., K.C.	7	10	4.74	21	112.0	129	35	62
Drummond, T., Min.	3	5	4.35	35	91.0	104	36	49
Edens, T., Mil.	4	5	4.45	35	89.0	89	33	40
Edwards, W., Chi.*	5	3	3.22	42	95.0	81	41	63
Eichhorn, M., Cal.	2	5	3.08	60	84.2	98	23	69
Erickson, S., Min.	8	4	2.87	19	113.0	108	51	53
Farr, S., K.C.	13	7	1.98	57	127.0	99	48	94
Farrell, J., Cle.	4	5	4.28	17	96.2	108	33	44
Fernandez, A., Chi.	5	5	3.80	13	87.2	89	34	61

Pitcher and Team	W	L	ERA	G	IP	H	BB	SO
Finley, C., Cal.*	18	9	2.40	32	236.0	210	81	177
Gibson, P., Det.*	5	4	3.05	61	97.1	99	44	56
Gleaton, J., Det.*	1	3	2.94	57	82.2	62	25	56
Gordon, T., K.C.	12	11	3.73	32	195.1	192	99	175
Gubicza, M., K.C.	4	7	4.50	16	94.0	101	38	71
Guetterman, L., N.Y.*	11	7	3.39	64	93.0	80	26	48
Guthrie, M., Min.*	7	9	3.79	24	144.2	154	39	101
Hanson, E., Sea.	18	9	3.24	33	236.0	205	68	211
Harnisch, P., Bal.	11	11	4.34	31	188.2	189	86	122
Harris, G., Bos.	13	9	4.00	34	184.1	186	77	117
Hawkins, A., N.Y.	5	12	5.37	28	157.2	156	82	74
Henneman, M., Det.	8	6	3.05	69	94.1	90	33	50
Hibbard, G., Chi.*	14	9	3.16	33	211.0	202	55	92
Higuera, T., Mil.*	11	10	3.76	27	170.0	167	50	129
Holman, B., Sea.	11	11	4.03	28	189.2	188	66	121
Hough, C., Tex.	12	12	4.07	32	218.2	190	119	114
Jeffcoat, M., Tex.*	5	6	4.47	44	110.2	122	28	58
Johnson, D., Bal.	13	9	4.10	30	180.0	196	43	68
Johnson, R., Sea.*	14	11	3.65	33	219.2	174	120	194
Jones, D., Cle.	5	5	2.56	66	84.1	66	22	55
Key, J., Tor.*	13	7	4.25	27	154.2	169	22	88
Kiecker, D., Bos.	8	9	3.97	32	152.0	145	54	93
King, E., Chi.	12	4	3.28	25	151.0	135	40	70
Knudson, M., Mil.	10	9	4.12	30	168.1	187	40	56
Krueger, B., Mil.*	6	8	3.98	30	129.0	137	54	64
LaPoint, D., N.Y.*	7	10	4.11	28	157.2	180	57	67
Lamp, D., Bos.	3	5	4.68	47	105.2	114	30	49
Langston, M., Cal.*	10	17	4.40	33	223.0	215	104	195
Leach, T., Min.	2	5	3.20	55	81.2	84	21	46
Leary, T., N.Y.	9	19	4.11	31	208.0	202	78	138
McCaskill, K., Cal.	12	11	3.25	29	174.1	161	72	78
McDonald, B., Bal.	8	5	2.43	21	118.2	88	35	65
McDowell, J., Chi.	14	9	3.82	33	205.0	189	77	165
Milacki, B., Bal.	5	8	4.46	27	135.1	143	61	60
Mitchell, J., Bal.	6	6	4.64	24	114.1	133	48	43
Montgomery, J., K.C.	6	5	2.39	73	94.1	81	34	94
Moore, M., Oak.	13	15	4.65	33	199.1	204	84	73

Pitcher and Team	W	L	ERA	G	IP	H	BB	SO
Morris, J., Det.	15	18	4.51	36	249.2	231	97	162
Moyer, J., Tex.*	2	6	4.66	33	102.1	115	39	58
Navarro, J., Mil.	8	7	4.46	32	149.1	176	41	75
Nunez, E., Det.	3	1	2.24	42	80.1	65	37	66
Olin, S., Cle.	4	4	3.41	50	92.1	96	26	64
Olson, G., Bal.	6	5	2.42	64	74.1	57	31	74
Orosco, J., Cle.*	5	4	3.90	55	64.2	58	38	55
Perez, M., Chi.	13	14	4.61	35	197.0	177	86	161
Peterson, A., Chi.	2	5	4.55	20	85.0	90	26	29
Petry, D., Det.	10	9	4.45	32	149.2	148	77	73
Robinson, J., N.Y.	3	6	3.45	54	88.2	82	34	43
Robinson, J., Det.	10	9	5.96	27	145.0	141	88	76
Robinson, R., Mil.	12	5	2.91	22	148.1	158	37	57
Rogers, K., Tex.*	10	6	3.13	69	97.2	93	42	74
Ryan, N., Tex.	13	9	3.44	30	204.0	137	74	232
Saberhagen, B., K.C.	5	9	3.27	20	135.0	146	28	87
Sanderson, S., Oak.	17	11	3.88	34	206.1	205	66	128
Smith, R., Min.	5	10	4.81	32	153.1	191	47	87
Stewart, D., Oak.	22	11	2.56	36	267.0	226	83	166
Stieb, D., Tor.	18	6	2.93	33	208.2	179	64	125
Stottlemyre, T., Tor.	13	17	4.34	33	203.0	214	69	115
Swift, B., Sea.	6	4	2.39	55	128.0	135	21	42
Swindell, G., Cle.*	12	9	4.40	34	214.2	245	47	135
Tanana, F., Det.*	9	8	5.31	34	176.1	190	66	114
Tapani, K., Min.	12	8	4.07	28	159.1	164	29	101
Thigpen, B., Chi.	4	6	1.83	77	88.2	60	32	70
Valdez, S., Cle.	6	6	4.75	24	102.1	109	35	63
Ward, D., Tor.	2	8	3.45	73	127.2	101	42	112
Welch, B., Oak.	27	6	2.95	35	238.0	214	77	127
Wells, D., Tor.*	11	6	3.14	43	189.0	165	45	115
West, D., Min.*	7	9	5.10	29	146.1	142	78	92
Williamson, M., Bal.	8	2	2.21	49	85.1	65	28	60
Wills, F., Tor.	6	4	4.73	44	99.0	101	38	72
Witt, B., Tex.	17	10	3.36	33	222.0	197	110	221
Witt, M., Cal.-N.Y.	5	9	4.00	26	117.0	106	47	74
Young, C., Oak.*	9	6	4.85	26	124.1	124	53	56
Young, M., Sea.*	8	18	3.51	34	225.1	198	107	176

NATIONAL LEAGUE
Batting

(42 or more at-bats)
*Bats Left-Handed   †Switch-Hitter

Batter and Team	AVG	G	AB	R	H	HR	RBI	SB
Abner, S., S.D.	.245	91	184	17	45	1	15	2
Aldrete, M., Mon.*	.242	96	161	22	39	1	18	1
Alomar, R., S.D.†	.287	147	586	80	168	6	60	24
Anderson, D., S.F.	.350	60	100	14	35	1	6	1
Anthony, E., Hou.*	.192	84	239	26	46	10	29	5
Armstrong, J., Cin.	.106	29	47	2	5	0	3	0
Backman, W., Pit.†	.292	104	315	62	92	2	28	6
Bass, K., S.F.†	.252	61	214	25	54	7	32	2
Bathe, B., S.F.	.229	52	48	3	11	3	12	0
Belcher, T., L.A.	.163	24	43	5	7	0	1	0
Bell, J., Pit.	.254	159	583	93	148	7	52	10
Bell, M., Atl.*	.244	36	45	8	11	1	5	0
Belliard, R., Pit.	.204	47	54	10	11	0	6	1
Benes, A., S.D.	.100	32	60	2	6	0	2	0
Benjamin, M., S.F.	.214	22	56	7	12	2	3	1
Benzinger, T., Cin.†	.253	118	376	35	95	5	46	3
Berryhill, D., Chi.†	.189	17	53	6	10	1	9	0
Bielecki, M., Chi.	.163	36	43	3	7	0	1	0
Biggio, C., Hou.	.276	150	555	53	153	4	42	25
Blauser, J., Atl.	.269	115	386	46	104	8	39	3
Bonds, B., Pit.*	.301	151	519	104	156	33	114	52
Bonilla, B., Pit.†	.280	160	625	112	175	32	120	4
Booker, R., Phi.*	.221	73	131	19	29	0	10	3
Boston, D., N.Y.*	.273	115	366	65	100	12	45	18
Boyd, D., Mon.	.051	31	59	1	3	0	0	0
Braggs, G., Cin.	.299	72	201	22	60	6	28	3
Bream, S., Pit.*	.270	147	389	39	105	15	67	8
Brooks, H., L.A.	.266	153	568	74	151	20	91	2
Browning, T., Cin.*	.093	38	75	6	7	0	4	0
Brunansky, T., St.L.	.158	19	57	5	9	1	2	0

Batter and Team	AVG	G	AB	R	H	HR	RBI	SB
Burkett, J., S.F.	.048	33	63	1	3	0	3	0
Butler, B., S.F.*	.309	160	622	108	192	3	44	51
Cabrera, F., Atl.	.277	63	137	14	38	7	25	1
Caminiti, K., Hou.†	.242	153	541	52	131	4	51	9
Campusano, S., Phi.	.212	66	85	10	18	2	9	1
Candaele, C., Hou.†	.286	130	262	30	75	3	22	7
Cangelosi, J., Pit.†	.197	58	76	13	15	0	1	7
Carreon, M., N.Y.	.250	82	188	30	47	10	26	1
Carter, G., S.F.	.254	92	244	24	62	9	27	1
Carter, J., S.D.	.232	162	634	79	147	24	115	22
Chamberlain, W., Phi.	.283	18	46	9	13	2	4	4
Clark, D., Chi.*	.275	84	171	22	47	5	20	7
Clark, Ja., S.D.	.266	115	334	59	89	25	62	4
Clark, Je., S.D.	.267	53	101	12	27	5	11	0
Clark, W., S.F.*	.295	154	600	91	177	19	95	8
Coleman, V., St.L.†	.292	124	497	73	145	6	39	77
Collins, D., St.L.†	.224	99	58	12	13	0	3	7
Combs, P., Phi.*	.150	32	60	6	9	0	2	0
Cone, D., N.Y.*	.200	32	70	7	14	0	5	0
Cook, D., Phi.-L.A.*	.306	48	49	8	15	1	4	0
Cora, J., S.D.†	.270	51	100	12	27	0	2	8
Daniels, K., L.A.*	.296	130	450	81	133	27	94	4
Dascenzo, D., Chi.†	.253	113	241	27	61	1	26	15
Daulton, D., Phi.*	.268	143	459	62	123	12	57	7
Davidson, M., Hou.	.292	57	130	12	38	1	11	0
Davis, E., Cin.	.260	127	453	84	118	24	86	21
Davis, G., Hou.	.251	93	327	44	82	22	64	8
Dawson, A., Chi.	.310	147	529	72	164	27	100	16
Decker, S., S.F.	.296	15	54	5	16	3	8	0
DeLeon, J., St.L.	.107	32	56	1	6	0	3	0
Dempsey, R., L.A.	.195	62	128	13	25	2	15	1
Deshaies, J., Hou.*	.063	34	63	1	4	0	3	0
DeShields, D., Mon.*	.289	129	499	69	144	4	45	42
Doran, B., Hou.-Cin.†	.300	126	403	59	121	7	37	23
Drabek, D., Pit.	.214	33	84	8	18	1	6	0
Duncan, M., Cin.	.306	125	435	67	133	10	55	13
Dunston, S., Chi.	.262	146	545	73	143	17	66	25

Batter and Team	AVG	G	AB	R	H	HR	RBI	SB
Dykstra, L., Phi.*	.325	149	590	106	192	9	60	33
Elster, K., N.Y.	.207	92	314	36	65	9	45	2
Fernandez, S., N.Y.*	.190	30	58	3	11	0	4	0
Fitzgerald, M., Mon.	.243	111	313	36	76	9	41	8
Foley, T., Mon.*	.213	73	164	11	35	0	12	0
Galarraga, A., Mon.	.256	155	579	65	148	20	87	10
Gant, R. Atl.	.303	152	575	107	174	32	84	33
Gardner, M., Mon.	.114	27	44	2	5	0	1	0
Garrelts, S., S.F.	.061	42	66	5	4	0	0	1
Gedman, R., Hou.*	.202	40	104	4	21	1	10	0
Gibson, K., L.A.*	.260	89	315	59	82	8	38	26
Gilkey, B., St.L.	.297	18	64	11	19	1	3	6
Girardi, J., Chi.	.270	133	419	36	113	1	38	8
Glavine, T., Atl.*	.113	34	62	5	7	0	4	0
Goff, J., Mon.*	.227	52	119	14	27	3	7	0
Gonzalez, J., L.A.	.232	106	99	15	23	2	8	3
Gooden, D., N.Y.	.187	35	75	4	14	1	9	0
Grace, M., Chi.	.309	157	589	72	182	9	82	15
Gregg, T., Atl.*	.264	124	239	18	63	5	32	4
Griffey, K., Cin.*	.206	46	63	6	13	1	8	2
Griffin, A., L.A.†	.210	141	461	38	97	1	35	6
Grissom, M., Mon.	.257	98	288	42	74	3	29	22
Gross, K., Mon.	.200	32	50	3	10	1	4	0
Guerrero, P., St.L.	.281	136	498	42	140	13	80	1
Gullickson, B., Hou.	.158	32	57	2	9	1	5	0
Gwynn, C., L.A.*	.284	101	141	19	40	5	22	0
Gwynn, T., S.D.*	.309	141	573	79	177	4	72	17
Harkey, M., Chi.	.250	27	56	4	14	0	4	0
Harris, L., L.A.*	.304	137	431	61	131	2	29	15
Hatcher, B., Cin.	.276	139	504	68	139	5	25	30
Hatcher, M., L.A.	.212	85	132	12	28	0	13	0
Hayes, C., Phi.	.258	152	561	56	145	10	57	4
Hayes, V., Phi.*	.261	129	467	70	122	17	73	16
Heaton, N., Pit.*	.047	32	43	3	2	0	1	1
Herr, T., Phi.-N.Y.†	.261	146	547	48	143	5	60	7
Hollins, D., Phi.†	.184	72	114	14	21	5	15	0
Howard, T., S.D.†	.273	20	44	4	12	0	0	0

Batter and Team	AVG	G	AB	R	H	HR	RBI	SB
Hudler, R., Mon.-St.L.	.282	93	220	31	62	7	22	18
Hundley, T., N.Y.†	.209	36	67	8	14	0	2	0
Hurst, B., S.D.†	.090	33	67	2	6	0	1	0
Jackson, D., S.D.	.257	58	113	10	29	3	9	3
Javier, S., L.A.†	.304	104	276	56	84	3	24	15
Jefferies, G., N.Y.†	.283	153	604	96	171	15	68	11
Johnson, H., N.Y.†	.244	154	590	89	144	23	90	34
Johnson, W., Mon.†	.163	47	49	6	8	1	5	1
Jones, R., Phi.*	.276	24	58	5	16	3	7	0
Jones, T., St.L.*	.219	67	128	9	28	1	12	3
Jordan, R., Phi.	.241	92	324	32	78	5	44	2
Jose, F., St.L.†	.271	25	85	12	23	3	13	4
Justice, D., Atl.*	.282	127	439	76	124	28	78	11
Kennedy, T., S.F.*	.277	107	303	25	84	2	26	1
King, J., Pit.	.245	127	371	46	91	14	53	3
Kingery, M., S.F.*	.295	105	207	24	61	0	24	6
Kremers, J., Atl.*	.110	29	73	7	8	1	2	0
Kruk, J., Phi.*	.291	142	443	52	129	7	67	10
Lake, S., Phi.	.250	29	80	4	20	0	6	0
Lampkin, T., S.D.*	.222	26	63	4	14	1	4	0
Lankford, R., St.L.*	.286	39	126	12	36	3	12	8
Larkin, B., Cin.	.301	158	614	85	185	7	67	30
LaValliere, M., Pit.*	.258	96	279	27	72	3	31	0
Leach, R., S.F.*	.293	78	174	24	51	2	16	0
Leibrandt, C., Atl.	.180	24	50	2	9	0	3	0
Lemke, M., Atl.†	.226	102	239	22	54	0	21	0
Lilliquist, D., Atl.-S.D.*	.256	29	43	6	11	2	3	0
Lind, J., Pit.	.261	152	514	46	134	1	48	8
Litton, G., S.F.	.245	93	204	17	50	1	24	1
Lynn, F., S.D.*	.240	90	196	18	47	6	23	2
Lyons, B., N.Y.-L.A.	.235	27	85	9	20	3	9	0
Maddux, G., Chi.	.145	35	83	1	12	0	3	0
Magadan, D., N.Y.*	.328	144	451	74	148	6	72	2
Magrane, J., St.L.	.127	31	55	3	7	0	0	0
Marshall, M., N.Y.	.239	53	163	24	39	6	27	0
Martinez, C., Phi.-Pit.	.240	83	217	26	52	10	35	2
Martinez, Da., Mon.*	.279	118	391	60	109	11	39	13

Batter and Team	AVG	G	AB	R	H	HR	RBI	SB
Martinez, De., Mon.	.103	32	68	0	7	0	6	0
Martinez, R., L.A.*	.125	33	80	2	10	0	6	0
May, D., Chi.*	.246	17	61	8	15	1	11	1
McClendon, L., Chi.-Pit. ...	.164	53	110	6	18	2	12	1
McDowell, O., Atl.*	.243	113	305	47	74	7	25	13
McGee, W., St.L.†	.335	125	501	76	168	3	62	28
McReynolds, K., N.Y.	.269	147	521	75	140	24	82	9
Mercado, O., N.Y.-Mon.	.214	50	98	10	21	3	7	0
Miller, K., N.Y.	.258	88	233	42	60	1	12	16
Mitchell, K., S.F.	.290	140	524	90	152	35	93	4
Morandini, M., Phi.*	.241	25	79	9	19	1	3	3
Morgan, M., L.A.	.113	33	71	2	8	0	2	0
Morris, H., Cin.*	.340	107	309	50	105	7	36	9
Mulholland, T., Phi.	.097	33	62	2	6	0	2	0
Murphy, D., Atl.-Phi.	.245	154	563	60	138	24	83	9
Murray, E., L.A.†	.330	155	558	96	184	26	95	8
Nichols, C., Hou.	.204	32	49	7	10	0	11	0
Nixon, O., Mon.†	.251	119	231	46	58	1	20	50
Noboa, J., Mon.	.266	81	158	15	42	0	14	4
Oberkfell, K., Hou.*	.207	77	150	10	31	1	12	1
O'Brien, C., N.Y.	.162	28	68	6	11	0	9	0
Oester, R., Cin.†	.299	64	154	10	46	0	13	1
Offerman, J., L.A.†	.155	29	58	7	9	1	7	1
Oliver, J., Cin.	.231	121	364	34	84	8	52	1
Olson, G., Atl.	.262	100	298	36	78	7	36	1
O'Malley, T., N.Y.*	.223	82	121	14	27	3	14	0
O'Neill, P., Cin.*	.270	145	503	59	136	16	78	13
Oquendo, J., St.L.†	.252	156	469	38	118	1	37	1
Ortiz, J., Hou.	.273	30	77	7	21	1	10	1
Owen, S., Mon.†	.234	149	453	55	106	5	35	8
Pagliarulo, M., S.D.*	.254	128	398	29	101	7	38	1
Pagnozzi, T., St.L.	.277	69	220	20	61	2	23	1
Parent, M., S.D.	.222	65	189	13	42	3	16	1
Parker, R., S.F.	.243	54	107	19	26	2	14	6
Pena, G., St.L.†	.244	18	45	5	11	0	2	1
Pendleton, T., St.L.†	.230	121	447	46	103	6	58	7
Portugal, M., Hou.	.136	32	66	2	9	0	5	0

Batter and Team	AVG	G	AB	R	H	HR	RBI	SB
Presley, J., Atl.	.242	140	541	59	131	19	72	1
Quinones, L., Cin.†	.241	83	145	10	35	2	17	1
Raines, T., Mon.†	.287	130	457	65	131	9	62	49
Ramirez, R., Hou.	.261	132	445	44	116	2	37	10
Ramos, D., Chi.	.265	98	226	22	60	2	17	0
Randolph, W., L.A.	.271	26	96	15	26	1	9	1
Rasmussen, D., S.D.*	.290	33	62	8	18	0	8	0
Ready, R., Phi.	.244	101	217	26	53	1	26	3
Redus, G., Pit.	.247	96	227	32	56	6	23	11
Reed, J., Cin.*	.251	72	175	12	44	3	16	0
Reynolds, R., Pit.†	.288	95	215	25	62	0	19	12
Rhodes, K., Hou.*	.244	38	86	12	21	1	3	4
Rijo, J., Cin.	.161	29	62	3	10	0	2	1
Riles, E., S.F.*	.200	92	155	22	31	8	21	0
Roberts, L., S.D.†	.309	149	556	104	172	9	44	46
Robinson, D., S.F.	.143	31	63	4	9	2	7	0
Rohde, D., Hou.†	.184	59	98	8	18	0	5	0
Roomes, R., Cin.-Mon. ...	.227	46	75	6	17	2	8	0
Ruffin, B., Phi.†	.068	32	44	3	3	0	0	0
Sabo, C., Cin.	.270	148	567	95	153	25	71	25
Salazar, L., Chi.	.254	115	410	44	104	12	47	3
Samuel, J., L.A.	.242	143	492	62	119	13	52	38
Sandberg, R., Chi.	.306	155	615	116	188	40	100	25
Santiago, B., S.D.	.270	100	344	42	93	11	53	5
Santovenia, N., Mon.	.190	59	163	13	31	6	28	0
Sasser, M., N.Y.*	.307	100	270	31	83	6	41	0
Scioscia, M., L.A.*	.264	135	435	46	115	12	66	4
Scott, M., Hou.	.130	32	54	0	7	0	1	1
Sharperson, M., L.A.	.297	129	357	42	106	3	36	15
Slaught, D., Pit.	.300	84	230	27	69	4	29	0
Smiley, J., Pit.*	.122	26	49	1	6	0	3	0
Smith, D., Chi.*	.262	117	290	34	76	6	27	11
Smith, G., Chi.†	.205	18	44	4	9	0	5	1
Smith, L., Atl.	.305	135	466	72	142	9	42	10
Smith, O., St.L.†	.254	143	512	61	130	1	50	32
Smith, Z., Mon.-Pit.*	.162	34	68	1	11	0	2	0
Smoltz, J., Atl.	.162	38	74	7	12	0	4	1

Batter and Team	AVG	G	AB	R	H	HR	RBI	SB
Stephenson, P., S.D.*	.209	103	182	26	38	4	19	2
Strawberry, D., N.Y.*	.277	152	542	92	150	37	108	15
Stubbs, F., Hou.*	.261	146	448	59	117	23	71	19
Tabler, P., N.Y.	.279	17	43	6	12	1	10	0
Templeton, G., S.D.†	.248	144	505	45	125	9	59	1
Teufel, T., N.Y.	.246	80	175	28	43	10	24	0
Thomas, A., Atl.	.219	84	278	26	61	5	30	2
Thompson, M., St.L.*	.218	135	418	42	91	6	30	25
Thompson, R., S.F.	.245	144	498	67	122	15	56	14
Thon, D., Phi.	.255	149	552	54	141	8	48	12
Treadway, J., Atl.*	.283	128	474	56	134	11	59	3
Trevino, A., Hou.-N.Y.-Cin.	.221	58	86	3	19	1	13	0
Tudor, J., St.L.*	.152	25	46	3	7	0	3	0
Uribe, J., S.F.†	.248	138	415	35	103	1	24	5
Valenzuela, F., L.A.*	.304	35	69	8	21	1	11	0
Van Slyke, A., Pit.*	.284	136	493	67	140	17	77	14
Varsho, G., Chi.*	.250	46	48	10	12	0	1	2
Vatcher, J., Phi.-Atl.	.260	57	73	7	19	1	7	0
Villanueva, H., Chi.	.272	52	114	14	31	7	18	1
Viola, F., N.Y.*	.153	35	85	4	13	0	4	0
Vizcaino, J., L.A.†	.275	37	51	3	14	0	2	1
Walker, L., Mon.*	.241	133	419	59	101	19	51	21
Wallach, T., Mon.	.296	161	626	69	185	21	98	6
Walling, D., St.L.*	.220	78	127	7	28	1	19	0
Walton, J., Chi.	.263	101	392	63	103	2	21	14
Whitson, E., S.D.	.149	33	67	6	10	1	4	0
Whitt, E., Atl.*	.172	67	180	14	31	2	10	0
Wilkerson, C., Chi.†	.220	77	186	21	41	0	16	2
Williams, E., S.D.	.286	14	42	5	12	3	4	0
Williams, M., S.F.	.277	159	617	87	171	33	122	7
Wilson, C., St.L.	.248	55	121	13	30	0	7	0
Wilson, G., Hou.	.245	118	368	42	90	10	55	0
Winningham, H., Cin.*	.256	84	160	20	41	3	17	6
Wynne, M., Chi.*	.204	92	186	21	38	4	19	3
Yelding, E., Hou.	.254	142	511	69	130	1	28	64
Young, G., Hou.†	.175	57	154	15	27	1	4	6
Zeile, T., St.L.	.244	144	495	62	121	15	57	2

NATIONAL LEAGUE
Pitching

(40 or more innings pitched)
*Throws Left-Handed

Pitcher and Team	W	L	ERA	G	IP	H	BB	SO
Agosto, J., Hou.*	9	8	4.29	82	92.1	91	39	50
Akerfelds, D., Phi.	5	2	3.77	71	93.0	65	54	42
Andersen, L., Hou.	5	2	1.95	50	73.2	61	24	68
Armstrong, J., Cin.	12	9	3.42	29	166.0	151	59	110
Assenmacher, P., Chi.*	7	2	2.80	74	103.0	90	36	95
Avery, S., Atl.*	3	11	5.64	21	99.0	121	45	75
Bedrosian, S., S.F.	9	9	4.20	68	79.1	72	44	43
Belcher, T., L.A.	9	9	4.00	24	153.0	136	48	102
Belinda, S., Pit.	3	4	3.55	55	58.1	48	29	55
Benes, A., S.D.	10	11	3.60	32	192.1	177	69	140
Bielecki, M., Chi.	8	11	4.93	36	168.0	188	70	103
Birtsas, T., Cin.*	1	3	3.86	29	51.1	69	24	41
Boever, J., Atl.-Phi.	3	6	3.36	67	88.1	77	51	75
Boskie, S., Chi.	5	6	3.69	15	97.2	99	31	49
Boyd, D., Mon.	10	6	2.93	31	190.2	164	52	113
Brantley, J., S.F.	5	3	1.56	55	86.2	77	33	61
Browning, T., Cin.*	15	9	3.80	35	227.2	235	52	99
Burke, T., Mon.	3	3	2.52	58	75.0	71	21	47
Burkett, J., S.F.	14	7	3.79	33	204.0	201	61	118
Carman, D., Phi.*	6	2	4.15	59	86.2	69	38	58
Castillo, T., Atl.*	5	1	4.23	52	76.2	93	20	64
Charlton, N., Cin.*	12	9	2.74	56	154.1	131	70	117
Clancy, J., Hou.	2	8	6.51	33	76.0	100	33	44
Clary, M., Atl.	1	10	5.67	33	101.2	128	39	44
Combs, P., Phi.*	10	10	4.07	32	183.1	179	86	108
Cone, D., N.Y.	14	10	3.23	31	211.2	177	65	233
Cook, D., Phi.-L.A.*	9	4	3.92	47	156.0	155	56	64
Crews, T., L.A.	4	5	2.77	66	107.1	98	24	76
Darling, R., N.Y.	7	9	4.50	33	126.0	135	44	99
Darwin, D., Hou.	11	4	2.21	48	162.2	136	31	109
Dayley, K., St.L.*	4	4	3.56	58	73.1	63	30	51

Pitcher and Team	W	L	ERA	G	IP	H	BB	SO
DeJesus, J., Phi.	7	8	3.74	22	130.0	97	73	87
DeLeon, J., St.L.	7	19	4.43	32	182.2	168	86	164
Deshales, J., Hou.*	7	12	3.78	34	209.1	186	84	119
Dibble, R., Cin.	8	3	1.74	68	98.0	62	34	136
DiPino, F., St.L.*	5	2	4.56	62	81.0	92	31	49
Downs, K., S.F.	3	2	3.43	13	63.0	56	20	31
Drabek, D., Pit.	22	6	2.76	33	231.1	190	56	131
Fernandez, S., N.Y.*	9	14	3.46	30	179.1	130	67	181
Franco, J., N.Y.*	5	3	2.53	55	67.2	66	21	56
Freeman, M., Phi.-Atl. ...	1	2	4.31	25	48.0	41	17	38
Frey, S., Mon.*	8	2	2.10	51	55.2	44	29	29
Gardner, M., Mon.	7	9	3.42	27	152.2	129	61	135
Garrelts, S., S.F.	12	11	4.15	31	182.0	190	70	80
Glavine, T., Atl.*	10	12	4.28	33	214.1	232	78	129
Gooden, D., N.Y.	19	7	3.83	34	232.2	229	70	223
Gott, J., L.A.	3	5	2.90	50	62.0	59	34	44
Grant, M., S.D.-Atl.	2	3	4.73	59	91.1	108	37	69
Greene, T., Atl.-Phi.	3	3	5.08	15	51.1	50	26	21
Grimsley, J., Phi.	3	2	3.30	11	57.1	47	43	41
Gross, K., Mon.	9	12	4.57	31	163.1	171	65	111
Gullickson, B., Hou.	10	14	3.82	32	193.1	221	61	73
Hall, D., Mon.*	4	7	5.09	42	58.1	52	29	40
Hammaker, A., S.F.-S.D.*	4	9	4.36	34	86.2	85	27	44
Harkey, M., Chi.	12	6	3.26	27	173.2	153	59	94
Harris, G., S.D.	8	8	2.30	73	117.1	92	49	97
Hartley, M., L.A.	6	3	2.95	32	79.1	58	30	76
Heaton, N., Pit.*	12	9	3.45	30	146.0	143	38	68
Hernandez, X., Hou.	2	1	4.62	34	62.1	60	24	24
Hill, K., St.L.	5	6	5.49	17	78.2	79	33	58
Horton, R., St.L.*	1	1	4.93	32	42.0	52	22	18
Howell, J., L.A.	5	5	2.18	45	66.0	59	20	59
Howell, K., Phi.	8	7	4.64	18	106.2	106	49	70
Hurst, B., S.D.*	11	9	3.14	33	223.2	188	63	162
Jackson, D., Cin.*	6	6	3.61	22	117.1	119	40	76
Kipper, B., Pit.*	5	2	3.02	41	62.2	44	26	35
Knepper, B., S.F.*	3	3	5.68	12	44.1	56	19	24
Kramer, R., Pit.-Chi.	0	3	4.50	22	46.0	47	21	27

Pitcher and Team	W	L	ERA	G	IP	H	BB	SO
LaCoss, M., S.F.	6	4	3.94	13	77.2	75	39	39
Lancaster, L., Chi.	9	5	4.62	55	109.0	121	40	65
Landrum, B., Pit.	7	3	2.13	54	71.2	69	21	39
Layana, T., Cin.	5	3	3.49	55	80.0	71	44	53
Lefferts, C., S.D.*	7	5	2.52	56	78.2	68	22	60
Leibrandt, C., Atl.*	9	11	3.16	24	162.1	164	35	76
Lilliquist, D., Atl.-S.D.* ..	5	11	5.31	28	122.0	136	42	63
Long, B., Chi.	6	1	4.37	42	55.2	66	21	32
Luecken, R., Atl.	1	4	5.77	36	53.0	73	30	35
Maddux, G., Chi. 15		15	3.46	35	237.0	242	71	144
Magrane, J., St.L.* 10		17	3.59	31	203.1	204	59	100
Mahler, R., Cin.	7	6	4.28	35	134.2	134	39	68
Marak, P., Atl.	1	2	3.69	7	39.0	39	19	15
Martinez, De., Mon. 10		11	2.95	32	226.0	191	49	156
Martinez, R., L.A. 20		6	2.92	33	234.1	191	67	223
Mathews, G., St.L.*	0	5	5.33	11	50.2	53	30	18
McDowell, R., Phi.	6	8	3.86	72	86.1	92	35	39
Mercker, K., Atl.*	4	7	3.17	36	48.1	43	24	39
Mohorcic, D., Mon.	1	2	3.23	34	53.0	56	18	29
Morgan, M., L.A. 11		15	3.75	33	211.0	216	60	106
Mulholland, T., Phi.*	9	10	3.34	33	180.2	172	42	75
Myers, R., Cin.*	4	6	2.08	66	86.2	59	38	98
Nabholz, C., Mon.*	6	2	2.83	11	70.0	43	32	53
Neidlinger, J., L.A.	5	3	3.28	12	74.0	67	15	46
Niedenfuer, T., St.L.	0	6	3.46	52	65.0	66	25	32
Nunez, J., Chi.	4	7	6.53	21	60.2	61	34	40
Ojeda, B., N.Y.*	7	6	3.66	38	118.0	123	40	62
Olivares, O., St.L.	1	1	2.92	9	49.1	45	17	20
Oliveras, F., S.F.	2	2	2.77	33	55.1	47	21	41
O'Neal, R., S.F.	1	0	3.83	26	47.0	58	18	30
Parrett, J., Phi.-Atl.	5	10	4.64	67	108.2	119	55	86
Patterson, B., Pit.*	8	5	2.95	55	94.2	88	21	70
Pena, A., N.Y.	3	3	3.20	52	76.0	71	22	76
Pico, J., Chi.	4	4	4.79	31	92.0	120	37	37
Portugal, M., Hou. 11		10	3.62	32	196.2	187	67	136
Power, T., Pit.	1	3	3.66	40	51.2	50	17	42
Rasmussen, D., S.D.* ...11		15	4.51	32	187.2	217	62	86

Pitcher and Team	W	L	ERA	G	IP	H	BB	SO
Reed, R., Pit.	2	3	4.36	13	53.2	62	12	27
Reuschel, R., S.F.	3	6	3.93	15	87.0	102	31	49
Rijo, J., Cin.	14	8	2.70	29	197.0	151	78	152
Robinson, D., S.F.	10	7	4.57	26	157.2	173	41	78
Rodriguez, R., S.D.*	1	1	2.83	32	47.2	52	16	22
Rojas, M., Mon.	3	1	3.60	23	40.0	34	24	26
Ruffin, B., Phi.*	6	13	5.38	32	149.0	178	62	79
Ruskin, S., Pit.-Mon.* ...	3	2	2.75	67	75.1	75	38	57
Sampen, B., Mon.	12	7	2.99	59	90.1	94	33	69
Schatzeder, D., Hou.-N.Y.*	1	3	2.20	51	69.2	66	23	39
Schiraldi, C., S.D.	3	8	4.41	42	104.0	105	60	74
Schmidt, D., Mon.	3	3	4.31	34	48.0	58	13	22
Scott, M., Hou.	9	13	3.81	32	205.2	194	66	121
Scudder, S., Cin.	5	5	4.90	21	71.2	74	30	42
Show, E., S.D.	6	8	5.76	39	106.1	131	41	55
Smiley, J., Pit.*	9	10	4.64	26	149.1	161	36	86
Smith, B., St.L.	9	8	4.27	26	141.1	160	30	78
Smith, D., Hou.	6	6	2.39	49	60.1	45	20	50
Smith, L., St.L.	3	4	2.10	53	68.2	58	20	70
Smith, P., Atl.	5	6	4.79	13	77.0	77	24	56
Smith, Z., Mon.-Pit.*	12	9	2.55	33	215.1	196	50	130
Smoltz, J., Atl.	14	11	3.85	34	231.1	206	90	170
Terrell, W., Pit.	2	7	5.88	16	82.2	98	33	34
Terry, S., St.L.	2	6	4.75	50	72.0	75	27	35
Tewksbury, B., St.L.	10	9	3.47	28	145.1	151	15	50
Thurmond, M., S.F.*	2	3	3.34	43	56.2	53	18	24
Tomlin, R., Pit.*	4	4	2.55	12	77.2	62	12	42
Tudor, J., St.L.*	12	4	2.40	25	146.1	120	30	63
Valenzuela, F., L.A.*	13	13	4.59	33	204.0	223	77	115
Viola, F., N.Y.*	20	12	2.67	35	249.2	227	60	182
Walk, B., Pit.	7	5	3.75	26	129.2	136	36	73
Wetteland, J., L.A.	2	4	4.81	22	43.0	44	17	36
Whitehurst, W., N.Y.	1	0	3.29	38	65.2	63	9	46
Whitson, E., S.D.	14	9	2.60	32	228.2	215	47	127
Williams, M., Chi.*	1	8	3.93	59	66.1	60	50	55
Wilson, S., Chi.*	4	9	4.79	45	139.0	140	43	95
Wilson, T., S.F.*	8	7	4.00	27	110.1	87	49	66

BRUCE WEBER PICKS
HOW THEY'LL FINISH IN 1991

American League East

1. Toronto
2. Boston
3. Baltimore
4. Cleveland
5. Detroit
6. New York
7. Milwaukee

American League West

1. Oakland
2. Texas
3. Chicago
4. Seattle
5. California
6. Minnesota
7. Kansas City

National League East

1. Chicago
2. New York
3. Pittsburgh
4. Philadelphia
5. Montreal
6. St. Louis

National League West

1. Los Angeles
2. San Francisco
3. Cincinnati
4. San Diego
5. Atlanta
6. Houston

American League Champions: Toronto
National League Champions: Los Angeles
World Champions: Toronto

YOU PICK
HOW THEY'LL FINISH IN 1991

**American League
East**

1.

2.

3.

4.

5.

6.

7.

**American League
West**

1.

2.

3.

4.

5.

6.

7.

**National League
East**

1.

2.

3.

4.

5.

6.

**National League
West**

1.

2.

3.

4.

5.

6.

American League Champions:

National League Champions:

World Champions: